JAHB:
Theoretical Wrestling Matches

Mike Spiritfair Marty

Get a JAHB, LLC: Milwaukee

Bibliographic Data

©2006 Michael Spiritfair Marty (Chapters 4-6)
 (Completion date: April 21, 2006)

All rights reserved. No part of this artistic expression may be used or reproduced in any manner whatsoever without prior written permission of the author, except in the case of brief quotations embodied in reviews.

Get a JAHB, LLC (Publisher)
Mike Spiritfair Marty (Imprint) is the author and arranger of this
 particular expression of the Word of God (for antitrust competitive purposes)

Cover art designer (2026):
Interior art illustrator (2026):

Library of Congress Cataloging-in-Publication Data
Names: Marty, Mike Spiritfair, author.
Title: Just another holy book / Mike Spiritfair Marty, BLS, BA, MBA.
Description: Get a JAHB paperback First Edition. | Milwaukee, WI : Get a JAHB, LLC, 2026.
Identifiers: LCCN 2025922294 | ISBN 9798998577352 (paperback)
Subjects: LCSH: Christianity--History--By period. The Bible--Modern texts and versions. Political science--Political theory--Consensus--Consent of the governed. Law--Religious law in general--Comparative religious law. Language and literature--Literature--Collections--Literary extracts. BISAC: BIBLES / Multiple Translations / Text | LAW / General | POLITICAL SCIENCE / Religion, Politics & State | RELIGION / Christian Theology / History
Classification: LCC BS125-198.B52 M32 2025 V2 | DDC 209.019 M32 V2

First Edition: Has general table of contents but no index

Dedication

Dedicated to Hus and Wycliffe (and Wayne)

Introduction

This holy remix of the Christian Bible is about one-eighth the length, and it employs excerpts from nine orthodox versions: King James (KJV), New American (NAB), New American Standard (NASB), New International (NIV), New King James (NKJV), Revised Standard (RSV), The Amplified (TAB), Today's English (TEV), and The Living (TLB).

A "+" has been placed in front of all verses in which one or more words have been changed from the original verse. A "+" has not been placed in front of verses in which only punctuation or capitalization has been altered nor in front of verses in which, for example, "Job" has been respelled as "Joebh," or in which YAH-way, God, Christ, He, or the LORD have been interchanged with each other. Sometimes, though, especially perhaps in the first two sections (History and Poetry), words have been mixed all around and their order changed, though the verse listing is intended to show in what way the words have been rearranged. If there are a lot of verse references for a short verse, presumably the word order has been significantly adjusted to create a particular idea.

Also, Tab 1 is for the setting, Tab 2 is for "God speaks," Tab 3 is for a human speaker, Tab 4 is for the adversarial spirit, and Tab 5 is for a human critic--generally, this is the structure.

This rearranged version is intended not to replace the Bible but to excite people to read their unabridged versions, though, ideally, *Just Another Holy Book* is an improvement in some aspects over the unabridged versions. A condensed work, however, is rarely, if ever, able to match the value of a great original.

Table of Contents

Bibliographic Data 2
Dedication 3
Introduction 4
Theoretical Wrestling Matches 8
Folly & Iniquity (FI) 9
  One 9
  Two 12
  Three 16
  Four 21
  Five 28
  Six 35
  Seven 39
Prophecy (Pr) 45
  One--Haggai 45
  Two 49
  Three 53
  Four 58
  Five 63
  Six--Habakkuk 70
  Seven 79
  Eight 84
  Nine 91
  Ten 97
  Eleven 101
Philosophy (Ph) 105
  One 105
  Two 109
  Three 114

    Four--Darius 116

    Five 122

    Six 127

    Seven--Zerubbabel 131

    Eight 137

    Nine 140

    Ten 145

    Eleven 150

    Twelve--The Preacher 153

Works Cited 157

    Folly & Iniquity 157

    Prophecy 159

    Philosophy 161

Just Another Holy Book (JAHB)

JAHB: Theoretical Wrestling Matches

-- 2 Esdras 14:47 (TEV)[1]

---
[1] *Holy*

Theoretical Wrestling Matches

-- *What Then Must We Do?*, Leo Tolstoy

-- Jeremiah 5:2-4 (New King James Version)[1]

---
[1] *Stricken*

Folly & Iniquity (FI)

One

1. Although the Law was in the hearts of the people, so also was the root of evil.

2. Some of them would speak and say, "Keep to yourself, do not come near me, for I am holier than you!" and so forth.

3. There were too many Israelites in the land of the living who had not directed their hearts to the God of their fathers--with the sanctuary in the center of their soul--and they were unfaithful and played the whore after the gods of the peoples of the land; especially those who were twenty years old and above.

+4. For according to their conduct they were hypocrites in their hearts.

5. "When you sent me to the LORD your God, saying, 'Pray for us to the LORD our God, and according to all that the YAH-way says, so declare to us and we will do it.' But you have not obeyed the voice of the LORD your God, as the duty of each day required."[2]

6. "Do not test the patience of the LORD. It is a snare for a man to devote rashly something as holy, and afterward to reconsider his vows."

7. "How long?"

8. "They shall be greatly ashamed who trust in carved images, who say to the molded images, 'You are our gods.'"

9. "My heart is overturned within me, for it is the land of carved images, and they are insane with their

---

[2] *Evil*

	idols."
+10.	"You have allowed their bellies to be filled, and they are satisfied. They shall leave their abundance to their children and favorite babes."
11.	"Precious as gold is the star of your gods, which you made for yourselves," says the LORD, whose name is the God of hosts.
12.	"He is not ashamed to pray to this lifeless thing about his marriage, his children, and his possessions. It is weak, but he prays to it for health. It is dead, but he prays to it for life. It has no experience, but he prays to[3] it for help. It cannot walk, but he prays to it for a successful journey. Its hands have no power, but he asks it to help him: in business, in making money, and in his work."
+13.	"And when they say, 'Seek out the wizard,' should they not instead seek their God, in whose sight we may find favor? Why seek the dead on behalf of the living?"
+14.	"For God will instruct and teach you properly, and speak soft words to you with a sound of gentle stillness and a delicate whispering voice."
15.	"God has given clear commandments to everyone coming into this world, telling them what they should do to obtain life and to avoid punishment. But the wicked would not listen and refused to obey him in what they do. They have made their own wicked and deceitful plans. They denied the existence of God Most High and refused to follow his ways."
16.	"The fool has said in his heart, 'There is no God, for there is no answer from God. Is the Spirit of the

---

[3] *Reconsider*

	LORD restricted?"[4]
+17.	"They acted proudly, and did not heed Your commandments, though a man will enhance his life if he obeys them. And they shrugged their shoulders, became stiff-necked, and would not hear."
18.	"They are corrupt, and have committed abominable injustice; there is no one who does good."
19.	"God looks down from heaven upon the children of men, to see if there is anyone who acts wisely, who seeks after God. They have all fallen away; they are all alike depraved. There is no one good, not even one."
+20.	"Because justice is never upheld, therefore the law is ineffective. For the wicked surround the righteous, and justice comes out perverted."
21.	"With their hearts bent on evil, people will sit at the same table and lie to each other."
+22.	"As a man loves cursing, may it come upon him. And when he takes no delight in blessing others, may blessings be far from him."[5]
23.	"Who will set a guard over my mouth, that my lips could be wisely sealed? It would keep me from making mistakes and prevent me from destroying myself with my own tongue! LORD, Father and Master of my life, do not leave me at the mercy of my own words; don't let them cause my downfall."
+24.	"O Lord, my Father, God of my life, do not let me be overcome by the lustful cravings of the flesh. Keep shameless passions away from my heart and do not

---

[4] *Business*
[5] *Corrupt*

let me look at others lasciviously."

25. "Whoever has no rule over his own spirit is like a city that is broken down and without walls."

26. "An angry man stirs up strife, and a furious man abounds in transgression."

27. "Wrath kills a foolish man, and envy slays a simple one."

28. "The simple believes every word, but the prudent man considers well his steps."[6]

+29. "Woe to those who call evil good, and good evil; who put darkness for light, and light for darkness; who put bitter for sweet, and sweet for bitter, for the Lord has poured out upon them a spirit of deep sleep."

Two

1. "This is what I commanded them, saying, 'Obey My voice, and I will be your God, and you shall be My people. Walk in all the ways I command you, that it may go well with you.'"

2. Yet they did not listen or obey, but walked in the counsels and in the imagination of their evil heart, and they went backward and not forward.

3. "I spoke to you in your times of prosperity, but you said, 'I will not hear.' This has been your manner from your youth, that you did not obey My voice."

4. "It is this day as it was in days of old."[7]

---

[6] *Lasciviously*
[7] *Imagination*

5. "And how many times shall I make you swear that you speak nothing but the truth in the name of the LORD? Amen and amen!"

6. "If you pamper your child and play with him, he will be a disappointment and a source of grief. Laugh with him now, and one day you will have to cry over him, grinding your teeth in regret."

7. "He who flees from fear shall fall into a trap, and he who gets out of the trap shall be caught in a snare."

8. "Wisdom crieth in the streets: How long, you simple ones, will you be naive? For scorners delight in their scorning, and fools hate knowledge. But if you turn at my reproof, surely I will pour out my spirit on you."

9. "I have called and you refused. I have offered my hand and no one regarded it. Because you disdained all my counsel, and would have none of my reproof, I also will laugh at your calamity."

+10. "If I speak to him ten times, yet he is not disturbed. He thinks he is[8] very clever while sitting safely in the house of his friends."

11. "When distress and anguish come upon you, then they will call on Me, but I will not answer. They will seek Me diligently, but they will not find Me, because they hated knowledge and did not choose the fear of the YAH-way. Therefore they shall eat the fruit of their own way."

+12. "But all who listen to Me shall live in peace, and will be secure, with no fear of being harmed."

13. "Because of laziness the building decays, and through idleness of hands the house leaks."

---

[8]*Disdained*

14. "In all labor there is profit, but idle chatter leads only to poverty."

+15. "A foolish person's mind works like a cartwheel. It veers like the wind and goes round and round in circles. So also is the laughter of a fool."

+16. "All of them speak words without worth or truth. There is no sincerity, everyone's mind is inconsistent, and they speak emptiness with[9] flattering lips and a double heart."

17. "A foolish or ungodly person causes a lifetime of grief. A sarcastic friend is like a wild horse that neighs no matter who tries to ride him."

18. "They grope in the darkness without light, and stagger like drunken men. They go nowhere and perish."

+19. "Their mouths speak empty words, their right hand is a right hand of falsehood, and they cannot even discern between an honest path and a path of lies."

20. "How long, O you sons of men, how long will you love worthlessness and seek falsehood?"

21. "Understand, you senseless among the people; and you fools, when will you be wise?"

+22. "The people will labor in vain, and they shall be weary from daybreak until the stars appear."[10]

+23. "Son of Man, you dwell in the midst of a rebellious community of people, which has eyes to see but does not see, and ears to hear but does not hear."

24. YAH-way says to them, "As you have done, it shall be

---

[9] *Cartwheel*
[10] *Sarcastic*

	done to you; your reprisal shall return upon your own head."
+25.	"The LORD still has not given you a heart of understanding, or eyes that see or ears that hear."
+26.	They had no respect for the YAH-way's commandments and would not live by them; they refused to be guided into the way of righteousness.
27.	"Their deeds will not allow them to turn to their God, and they do not know the LORD."
28.	"The LORD of hosts has treated all of us according to our ways and deeds."
29.	"At the window of my house I looked out through the lattice, and saw[11] among the simple youths a young man devoid of understanding. He was walking along the street near the corner where a certain woman lived. He was passing near her house in the evening after it was dark. And behold, the woman comes to meet him, robed as a harlot with a cunning heart."
30.	"She is loud and defiant. Her feet do not remain at home. She is now in the streets, now in the squares, and lurks by every corner. She seizes him and kisses him, and says, 'I have come out to meet you, to seek your presence earnestly, and I have found you.'"
31.	"'I have spread my couch with coverings, with colored linens of Egypt. I have sprinkled my bed with myrrh, aloes and cinnamon. Come, let us drink our fill of love until morning. Let us delight ourselves with caresses.'"
32.	"'For my man is not at home. He has gone on a long journey. He has taken a bag of money with

---

[11] *Lattice*

	him. Not till the full moon will he return home.' She wins him over by her repeated urging, with her smooth lips she leads him astray. He follows her stupidly, like an ox that is led to[12] slaughter, like a deer prancing into a trap, like a bird darting into a snare. He does not know that it will cost him his life."
33.	"A bad wife will make her husband gloomy and depressed. She treats her young harshly, as though they were not hers. Her labor is in vain, without concern, because God deprived her of wisdom, and did not endow her with understanding. Show me a timid man who can never make up his mind, and I will show you a wife who doesn't make her husband happy."
+34.	"Woe to him who gives drink to a woman, pouring it from the wineskin till she is drunk, so that he can gaze at her naked body--for she will despise him in her heart. And he is to blame, for he teaches her to hate him."
+35.	"My face is flushed from weeping! Let us search out and examine our ways, and turn back to the LORD, so that we will lack nothing for each day while we are bound in the bundle of the living."[13]

Three

+1.	"Being too busy causes many worries, and makes it difficult to sleep because a person's mind has to work overtime at night."

---

[12] *Cunning*
[13] *Timid*

2. "Like a man who catches at shadows or chases the wind, is the one who believes in dreams. Dreams have misled many people; they put their faith in them, only to be disappointed. For in many dreams and in many words there is nonsense."

3. "I know that the Spirit of the Holy God is in you. Why then do you behave with complete nonsense?"

4. "People of Israel, how foolish can you be? You haven't even tried to find out the truth."

5. "Do not say, 'Why were the former days better than these?' For it is not wise to ask this."

6. "If you have been foolish in exalting yourself, admit when you are wrong and you will avoid embarrassment."[14]

7. "Using force to get a point across is like a castrated man trying to rape a girl."

8. "Like a lame man's legs, which hang useless, so is a proverb in the mouth of fools."

9. "Money is a trap for those who are fascinated by it, a trap that every fool falls into."

10. "As a partridge that hatches eggs which it has not laid, so is he who makes a fortune, but unjustly."

11. "A man who borrows money to build a house is just collecting stones for his own tomb."

12. "I have taken all this to my heart and explain it that righteous men, wise men, and their deeds are in the hand of God. Love from hatred man cannot tell; both appear equally vain. There is one fate for the just and for the wicked, for the good and the bad: as it is for the good man, so it is for the sinner; as it is

---

[14]Nonsense

for him who swears rashly, so it is for him who[15] fears an oath. Among all the things that happen under the sun, this is the worst, that things turn out the same for all."

13. "Is it of the LORD or is it not of the LORD that the peoples labor to feed the fire and weary themselves in vain?"

14. "Who has woe? Who has sorrow? Who has contentions? Who has complaints? Who has wounds without cause? Who has redness of eyes? Those who linger long at the wine, those who go in search of mixed wine. Do not look on the wine when it is red, when it sparkles in the cup, when it swirls around smoothly. At the last it bites like a serpent, and stings like a viper. You will see hallucinations, and you will not be able to think or speak clearly. You will be like one sleeping in the midst of the sea, saying, 'I was struck. They have beaten me, but I did not feel it. When will I wake up? I need another drink!'"

+15. "When he sins by his drinking, he cannot stay at home. He enlarges his desire like hell, and a man and his father will go in to the same girl. His lust is like death, and cannot be satisfied."[16]

16. "Worst of all wounds are those of the heart, worst of all evils are the troubles that women cause."

17. "He who tills his land will have plenty of bread, but he who follows frivolity will have poverty enough!"

18. "Wine is a mocker, intoxicating drink arouses brawling, and whoever is led astray by it is not wise."

---

[15] *Fascinated*
[16] *Linger*

19.	"The righteous should choose his friends carefully, for the way of the wicked leads them astray."
20.	"Whoever is a partner with a thief hates his own life."
+21.	"Their lies cause them to stray from the path of righteousness."
22.	"The lip of truth shall be established for ever, but a lying tongue is only for a moment."
23.	"The wicked borrows and does not repay, but the righteous shows mercy[17] and gives."
+24.	"A little bit that a righteous person owns is a more pleasing possession than the riches of many evil people."
+25.	"It is vain for you to rise up early and stay up late--laboring endlessly--for the LORD gives sleep to those he loves."
26.	"The path of the just is like the shining sun, that shines ever brighter unto the perfect day."
27.	"The way of the wicked is like darkness; they do not know what makes them stumble."
+28.	"He made a pit and dug it out, and has fallen into the net which he hid and the ditch which he has made."
29.	"The words of his mouth are empty and deceitful. He has ceased to be wise and to do good."[18]
+30.	Though these haters of the LORD would often pretend submission to Him, still the people acted corruptly.

---

[17] *Astray*
[18] *Ditch*

+31. "Many people become increasingly arrogant when honors are given to them and favors are done for them. They do not know what to do with so much good fortune. They are never grateful."

32. "Their eyes bulge with abundance. They have more than heart could wish."

33. "The more they increased, the more they sinned against Me."

+34. "As dead flies cause a perfumer's ointment to give off a foul odor, so also does a little folly to one respected for honesty and prudence."

35. "They do not consider in their hearts. Now their own deeds have surrounded them. In proportion to the vileness of their sins I have dealt with them, and hidden My face from them."

+36. "Do not contaminate yourselves with any of these things, for by these[19] things the nations of the world are defiled. I will punish their iniquities and vomit them out of the land. You should therefore keep all of My commandments, and not only you, but also all foreigners living among you."

+37. The people whose ways the Jews admired and whose customs they tried to imitate often became their enemies and oppressed them. It is a serious error to disregard the Law of God.

---

[19] *Haters*

Four

+1. "O house of Israel," thus says the Lord GOD: "Go, serve your idols if you will not obey Me, but pollute ye My holy name no more with contributions from your storehouses full of plunder."

+2. These men have set up idols in their hearts, and they also contrive to place in front of themselves assorted means by which they will stumble into iniquity.[20]

3. "Yet I have reserved seven thousand in Israel, all whose knees have not bowed to the false idols of Baal, and every mouth that has not kissed them."

4. For idols speak delusion, and the diviners see lying visions and tell false dreams. The comfort they offer is useless. Therefore the people wander like sheep. They hurt, because there is no shepherd.

+5. They pursue the east wind continually. They feed on it daily and increase hypocrisy and the ruining of themselves by violent behavior.

6. They sow the wind, and reap the whirlwind.

7. "You shall eat, but not be satisfied; emptiness shall be in your midst."

8. They sell the righteous for silver, and the poor for a pair of sandals.

9. They have given a boy in exchange for a harlot, and sold a girl for wine, that they may drink.[21]

+10. And the leaders of Israel did not walk in the YAH-way, for they were greedy for money, and they accepted bribes and

---

[20] *Contrive*
[21] *Whirlwind*

were very corrupt in the administration of justice.

11. They practiced divination and magic and consulted fortunetellers and mediums. They sinned greatly against the LORD and stirred up his anger.

12. When they died, even if they died in severe pain, they departed to no one's sorrow.

+13. The Most High God often allows the lowest of men to rule over the kingdoms of mankind.

14. They delight in lies. They bless with their mouth, but they curse inwardly. And they abhor the one who speaks uprightly.

15. Each one flatters himself in his own eyes. He sets himself in a way that is not good. He does not reject evil.[22]

16. "Even though the inclination of the hearts of all people is unjust--as long as the earth remains, there will be springtime and harvest, cold and heat, winter and summer, day and night. And I will establish My covenant with you. Then you shall know that I am the LORD, that you may remember and be utterly silenced for shame when I pardon you for all the evil in your life," says the Lord GOD.

17. There is no truth or mercy or knowledge of God in the land. The people make promises and break them. They lie, steal, and commit adultery. Crimes increase, and there is one murder after another.

+18. "Because you have plundered the nations, they shall plunder you in return, and there will be vileness and violence for everyone in every city on the whole earth."

19. For the rich men of the city exploit the poor, her residents speak lies, and their tongue is deceitful in their mouth.

---

[22]Fortunetellers

20. Indeed, though his face is covered with fat, and his waist is heavy, God will send leanness into their souls.[23]

21. "He who hates reproof is stupid."

+22. "Surely, your people in your midst are as frightened as women!"

23. "There is another serious problem I have seen everywhere--riches being hoarded to the harm of its owner."

24. "Sinners!! They make a king glad with their wickedness, and princes with their lies. They are all adulterers, like an oven heated by a baker. They prepare their heart like an oven. In the morning it burns like a flaming fire."

+25. "You give beauty preparations to the women, and then you buy them for yourselves for fifteen shekels of silver, or one and one-half homers of barley."

26. The eye of an adulterer waits for the twilight.

27. He says, "No eye will see me."[24]

28. He disguises his face. In the dark they break into houses which they marked for themselves in the daytime.

+29. The night monster immodestly loosens the maiden's girdle, strips her of her clothes, shamefully exposes her thighs, and disgracefully violates her body.

30. "Let her be alone, for her soul is in deep distress."

31. Each one knows the plague of his own heart.

32. For the dark places of the earth are full of the habitations of cruelty.

---

[23] *Springtime*
[24] *Hoarded*

33.	"In your filthiness is lewdness. You have enraged Me by all these things. Behold, I in turn will bring your conduct down on your own head," declares the Lord GOD.
+34.	"You must not be covert in your lewdness. The harm this creates is greater than all your other bad behavior."[25]
+35.	"Because of your iniquity you will waste away. The supply of bread in Jerusalem will run short. They shall eat bread by weight and with anxiety, and shall drink water by measure and with dread, and be dismayed with one another."
36.	"I have created you. Why do you pretend to be another person?"
37.	"You invent a false vision in your own heart."
38.	"Would you condemn Me that you may be justified?"
39.	"You forgers of lies; you are all worthless physicians. Oh, that you would be silent, and it would be your wisdom!"
+40.	"Behold, the days are coming that a famine will be on the land. Not a famine of bread, nor a thirst for water, but of hearing the words of the YAH-way. You shall wander from sea to sea, and from north to east; you shall run to and fro, looking for it, but it shall not be found."
41.	"For son dishonors father, daughter rises against her mother,[26] daughter-in-law against her mother-in-law; a man's enemies are the men of his own house."
42.	"To recognize faces is never good. Giving preferred

---

[25] *Monster*
[26] *Forgers*

treatment to rich people is a clear case of selling one's soul for a piece of bread."

43. "The lost far outnumber those who are saved--it is like a wave compared with a drop of water."

44. "They pant after the dust of the earth which is on the head of the poor."

+45. With continual noise--Was it joy or weeping?--as with the voice of doves, beating their breasts, the children of Israel came to seek the LORD their God. They asked the way to Zion and looked toward it.

46. "Come and let us join ourselves to the LORD in a perpetual covenant that will not be forgotten."

47. "What? Even now! Whoever believes will not act hastily. Also I will[27] make justice the measuring line, and righteousness the plummet. The hail will sweep away the refuge of lies, and floods will destroy the secret place. Your covenant with death will be annulled, and your agreement with Sheol will be canceled."

48. "You who love the LORD, hate evil in your own life."

49. "Do no unrighteousness and speak no lies."

50. "And the sanctuary of the temple on the ascending highway shall be in the center of you."

51. "Do true: this is the first of the ways of God."

52. Then the priests answered and said, "No."

+53. "You also say, 'Oh, how tiresome to obey the Lord's way--what a weariness!' And you snub Me with a sniffle."

---

[27] *Wave*

54.	"For they are a people who err in their heart. Therefore their Maker[28] will not have compassion on them, and their Creator will not be gracious to them."
55.	"Everyone is brutish, lacking in knowledge."
56.	"And fear is on every side."
+57.	"They punish a man for a single word he has spoken, and they defraud a person of justice by meaningless arguments, that they may pile sin on top of sin on top of sin."
+58.	"Even the expressions on their faces testify against them, as they display their sin like Sodom. Woe to their souls! For they bring disaster upon themselves."
59.	"For Jerusalem has stumbled, and Judah is fallen, because their tongue and their doings are against the LORD."
60.	"To what purpose is the multitude of your sacrifices to Me? I do not delight in the blood of bulls, or of lambs or goats. I have had enough.[29] When you come to appear before Me, who has required this from your hand? Bring no more futile sacrifices. I cannot stand your New Moon Festivals, your Sabbaths, and your religious gatherings; they are all corrupted by your sins. Your appointed feasts My soul hates. They have become a burden to Me."
+61.	Then the LORD saw that the earth was violent and corrupt, and that the wickedness of mankind was great, and that every intent of the thoughts of their hearts was only evil continually. And YAH-way was sorry and grieved.

---

[28] *Unrighteousness*
[29] *Arguments*

62. "How long do you refuse to keep My commandments and My laws?"

63. "They have done nothing of all that You commanded them to do, or of which the LORD had said to them, 'You shall not do this thing.'"

64. They feared the LORD, yet served their own gods.

65. They followed idols and became vain. They imitated the nations around them although the LORD had said, "Do not do as they do."[30]

66. And they caused their sons and daughters to pass through the fire, practiced witchcraft and soothsaying, and sold themselves to do wickedness in the sight of the YAH-way.

+67. The idolatrous priests burned incense to the sun, to the moon, and to the constellations of the Zodiac.

68. "You have devoted yourself completely to doing what is wrong."

69. "You trust in lying words that cannot benefit you. Will you steal, murder, come into women not your wife, swear falsely, burn incense to Baal, and walk after other gods, then dare to stand before Me in My house, and say, 'We are saved! We are free to do these things'?"

70. "Has this house become a den of thieves? Behold, I have seen it," says the LORD.

71. They lie down by every altar on clothes taken in pledge, and drink the wine of those punished by fines in the house of their god.[31]

+72. They talk about the God of Jerusalem in the same way that they make fun of the gods and man-made idols from other

---

[30] *Religious*
[31] *Zodiac*

lands.

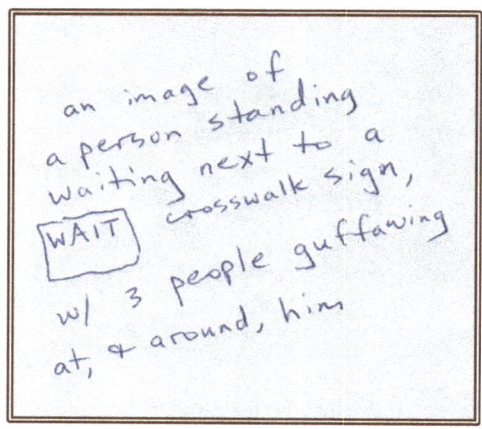

Five

1. "I want you to listen to me. Let me tell you what I think."

2. "There is a just man who perishes in his righteousness, and there is a wicked man who prolongs his life by sin."

3. "The race is not to the swift or the battle to the strong, nor does food come to the wise or wealth to the brilliant or favor to men of ability. But time and chance happen to them all."

4. "I looked for sympathy and loving-kindness, but there was none; and for comforters, but I found none."

5. "A feast is made for laughter, and wine gladdens life, and money is the[32] answer to

---
[32] *Sympathy*

	everything."
6.	"Whatever one is, he has been named already, for it is known that he is man. And he cannot contend with Him who is mightier than he. Since there are many things that increase frustration, what profit is there for a man? For who knows what is good for man in life, all the days of his futile life which he passes like a shadow?"
7.	"Listen to me. I also will declare my opinion."
8.	"Pride has its beginning when a person abandons the Lord, his Maker."
+9.	"Alas, the uproar of many people, and the rumbling of noisy nations who rush, rush, rush."
10.	"With misspent toil the potter molds a meaningless god from the soft clay. His concern is not that he is to die nor that his span of life is brief. Rather, he vies with goldsmiths and silversmiths and emulates molders of bronze, and takes pride in modeling counterfeits. His heart is made of ashes. His hope is cheaper than dirt. His life is not worth as much as[33] his clay, because he never came to know the God who shaped him, who breathed into him an active soul and a living spirit. He esteemed our life a plaything, a market where he can make money however he can, even by evil."
11.	"Will a person rob God? Yet you have robbed Me! But you say, 'In what way have we robbed you?'"
12.	"Return to Me, and I will return to you," says the LORD of hosts. "But you said, 'How?'"
13.	"Your attitude toward Me has been proud and arrogant," says the LORD.

---

[33] *Uproar*

14.	"I will not argue with your accusation."
+15.	"In the past I shared my morsels of food with the orphans."
16.	"But now I say, It is vain to serve God. What gain is it to obey the YAH-way and mourn for our sins?"[34]
17.	"So now we call the proud blessed. Not only are the doers of wickedness esteemed highly, but they also tempt the LORD and go free."
+18.	"Look at the iniquity of our sister Sodom. She didn't strengthen the hand of the poor and needy. And she had pride. But she also had fullness of food and abundance of leisure."
19.	"When vileness is exalted among the sons of men, the wicked prowl on every side in the Territory of Wickedness."
20.	"The children of sinners, brought up in ungodly surroundings, turn out to be hateful people."
21.	"Listen to me. I too will tell what I think."
22.	"A harlot is a deep pit, and a seductress is a narrow well. She also lies in wait as for a victim, and increases the unfaithful among men."
23.	"A drunken woman is an infuriating sight. She can't conceal her[35] shameless behavior."
24.	"A priest's daughter who loses her honor by

---

[34] *Plaything*
[35] *Prowl*

	committing fornication disgraces her father."
25.	"And the contentions of a wife are a continual dripping of rain."
+26.	"Is our strength like a stone, our flesh like bronze, that we may oppose the inclinations of nature? For who teaches us more than the beasts of the earth, and who is wiser than the birds of the air?"
+27.	"Be that as it may, a woman's beauty will warp your judgment, and lust has corrupted your thinking."
+28.	"If a father has a virgin daughter, he worries that she might be seduced and become pregnant while living in his house. If she is married, he worries that she might not be able to have children, or that she might be unfaithful."
29.	"You can tell an unfaithful wife by the bold and flirting look in her[36] eyes."
30.	"King Solomon loved many foreign women. Besides the daughter of the king of Egypt, he married Hittite women and women from Moab, Ammon, Edom, and Sidon. He married them even though the LORD had commanded the Israelites not to intermarry with these people, because they would cause the Israelites to give their loyalty to other gods. Solomon married seven hundred princesses and also had three hundred concubines. They made him turn away from God, and by the time he was old he was not faithful to the YAH-way."
31.	"Yes, the heart is deceitful above all things, and

---

[36] *Bronze*

	desperately wicked. Who can understand it?"
32.	"The rulers of Jerusalem judge for a bribe, her priests teach for pay, and her prophets preach for silver. Yet they lean on the LORD, and say 'Is not the LORD here with us?'"
33.	"Yes, these also have erred through wine, and through intoxicating drink have lost their way. They err in vision and stumble in judgment."[37]
34.	"Now therefore, look! The LORD has put a lying spirit in the mouth of all these prophets of yours."
35.	"And thus it is: because the priests are wicked, so too are the people."
36.	"From the least of them even to the greatest of them, everyone tries to make money dishonestly. And from the prophet even to the priest, everyone deals falsely. They have also healed the hurt of the daughters of My people superficially, saying 'Peace, peace!' when there is no peace."
+37.	"The priests feed on the sins of My people, and drink up their iniquities like water. By the peoples' sins, the priests get rich."
38.	"What has My beloved to do in My house, having done lewd deeds with many? And the holy flesh has passed from you. When you do evil, then you rejoice."
39.	"An astonishing and horrible thing has been committed in the land: the prophets prophesy falsely, and the priests rule by their own power.[38] And My people love to have it so. But what will you do in the end?"
40.	"For I know your manifold sins. You are the enemies of everything good. You oppress the righteous and take

---

[37] *Desperately*
[38] *Superficially*

bribes, and you deprive the poor of justice. Therefore the prudent man keeps quiet, for the times are full of lies and robbery."

41. "The wicked are like the troubled sea, when it cannot rest, whose waters cast up mire and dirt. There is no peace," says the LORD, "for the wicked."

42. "He who sows injustice will reap calamity."

43. "Someone with a guilty conscience will always imagine things to be worse than they really are. Fear is nothing but the failure to use the help that reason gives. When you lack the confidence to rely on reason, you give in to the fears caused by ignorance."

44. "For they who supposed their secret sins were hid under the dark veil of oblivion, now were scattered in fearful trembling, terrified by[39] apparitions. Not even the dark corners where they lay could protect them from fear. They were surrounded by horrible noises and grim ghosts."

+45. "Nothing was able to give them light, nor could the flaming brilliance of the stars succeed in relieving their deathly darkness."

46. "The illusions produced by their magic tricks were put to shame, and all the wisdom they had boasted of came to nothing. They had claimed they could drive away all the fears and illnesses of sick minds, but now they themselves were sick with silly, groundless fears."

+47. "All through their lives, they are angry, jealous, and in trouble. Small things disturb them, and they live with furious conflicts and with the fear of death. They think up new troubles in their sleep, and get little rest, if any at all. When they sleep, they are

---

[39] *Oblivion*

	restless, as if they were awake, and panicked by the sighing of the wind or by the singing of birds in the trees or by the roar of rushing water or by the rumble of falling rock or by the sound of unseen creatures running about or by the savage roaring of wild animals or by the echoes from the mountains."[40]
+48.	"If they dream that they are running from an enemy, just as they are about to be caught, they wake up and are astonished that there was nothing to fear."
+49.	"Such a person casts off all pity, and their anger tears at them perpetually."
50.	"'Changes and war are ever with me,' so they say."
51.	"Hell and Destruction are never full; so also the eyes of men and women are never satisfied."
52.	"Woe to him who increases what is not his--how long? And to him who loads himself with many pledges--will not your creditors rise up suddenly? And you will become their booty."
53.	"It shall even be as when a hungry man dreams. And look--he eats, but he awakes and his soul is still empty. Or as when a thirsty man dreams. And look--he drinks, but he awakes and indeed he is faint, and his soul still craves."[41]

Six....

1.	"Listen to me. I also will give you my opinion."

---

[40] *Illusions*
[41] *Perpetually*

2. "I think your tremendous statements are platitudes of ashes, and your defenses are defenses of clay."

3. "How long will the wicked triumph?"

4. "For I envied the arrogant, when I saw the prosperity of the wicked."

5. "And I said in myself, It is better for me to die than to live."

6. "So I said to God, 'O LORD, please take my life from me.'"

7. "Who is this who darkens counsel by words without knowledge?"

+8. "Don't you know that those who enjoy evil will have it with them into their old age? For the YAH-way catches the clever in their own craftiness."[42]

9. "Let them be caught in the plots which they have devised."

10. "For the King of Heaven is able to take those who walk in pride and debase them."

+11. "I say listen to me. Let me also declare my woman's perspective."

12. "Woe to you who plunder, though you have not been plundered. Woe to you who deal treacherously, though they have not dealt treacherously with you! When you cease plundering, you will be plundered. And as soon as you stop dealing treacherously, others shall deal treacherously with you."

---

[42] *Platitudes*

13.	"They do evil successfully with both hands. The governor and judge alike demand bribes. The rich man pays them off and tells them whom to ruin. They plot together."
14.	"The loyal man has perished from the earth, and there is no one upright among men."[43]
+15.	"The best of them is like the prickly stem of a rose; the most upright is sharper than a thorn bush."
16.	"They have rewarded me evil for good, and hatred for my love."
+17.	"Truth has stumbled in the streets, and honesty cannot enter. Truthfulness is nowhere to be found. Anyone who stops doing evil becomes a victim."
18.	The word of the LORD was rare in these days. There was no widespread revelation.
+19.	"Now listen to me awhile, and let me express my thoughts."
20.	"As long as you have been in this world, you have ruled it through terror, oppression, and deceit, with a total disregard for truth. You have viciously attacked harmless people who were living in peace. You have hated those who spoke the truth, and you have loved liars. You have destroyed the homes of those who were prosperous and have torn down the walls of those who did you no harm."[44]
21.	"Behold, the LORD's hand is not shortened, that it cannot save, nor His ear heavy, that it cannot hear. But your iniquities have separated you from your

---

[43] *Demand*
[44] *Prickly*

	God. And your sins have hidden His face from you, so that He will not hear."
22.	"For your hands are stained with blood, and your fingers with guilt. You lie and oppose the good. Your tongue has muttered perversity."
23.	"No one cares about being fair and true. Your lawsuits are based on unjust pleas."
24.	"They trust in confusion, conceive mischief and bring forth malice."
25.	"Their thoughts are thoughts of iniquity. Their works are works of iniquity and violence."
26.	"They do not know the way of peace. There is no justice in their paths. They have turned them into crooked roads."
27.	"Therefore justice is far from us, nor does righteousness overtake us.[45] We look for light, but there is darkness! For brightness, but we walk in blackness! We grope for the wall like the blind, and we grope as if we had no eyes. We stumble at noonday as at twilight. We are as dead men."
28.	"We all growl like bears, and moan sadly like doves. We look for justice, but there is none; for salvation, but it is far from us. For our transgressions are multiplied before You, and our sins testify against us. For our transgressions are with us, and as for our iniquities, we know what they are."
29.	"In transgressing and lying against the LORD, and departing from our God, speaking oppression and revolt, conceiving and uttering from the heart words of falsehood, justice is turned back, and righteousness stands afar off."

---

[45] *Oppose*

+30.   "He will not even hear our cries because of our demonic demeanor."

31.   "The tumult of those who rise up against You increases continually."[46]

32.   "I have sinned, for I have transgressed the commandment of the LORD, because I feared the people and obeyed their voice."

+33. He did evil, because he did not prepare his heart to seek the YAH-way way.

+34.   "Many of those who sleep in the dust of the earth shall awake, some to unlimited life, some to unlimited shame and contempt."

35.   "Why do the wicked renounce God? They have said in their heart, 'You will not require an account.'"

36. But because he became proud, stubborn, and cruel, he was removed from his royal throne and lost his place of honor.

37. He finally came to his senses and gave up his arrogant pride.

38.   At the same time my reason returned to me. "I have sinned. Indeed I have played the fool and erred exceedingly. Such things should not happen, nor be."[47]

39.   "We lie down in our shame, and our reproach covers us. For we have sinned against the LORD our God, we and our fathers, from our youth even to this day, and have not obeyed the voice of the YAH-way."

+40. To the wicked, God says, "What right have you to recite My statutes, and profess My covenant with your mouth? For you hate My instruction and disregard My laws."

---

[46] *Revolt*
[47] *Renounce*

41. Say to them, "This is a nation that does not obey the voice of the LORD their God; she refuses to be taught. Truth is dead and has vanished from their lips."

42. "You say, 'We have made a covenant with death, and with Sheol we are in agreement. For we have made lies our refuge, and under falsehood we have hidden ourselves.'"

43. "The womb of the wicked hatches mischief and iniquity. They tell lies from the day they are born."

44. "Don't trust anyone. Don't believe your neighbor or your friend. Your[48] wife lies to you even while in your embrace. Be careful what you say to her."

Seven

+1. "Woe to you who call the fool a gentleman, or the trickster an honest man."

+2. "For the fool does inequity, and his heart speaks nonsense. They practice ungodliness and utter error against the YAH-way, and they keep the hungry unsatisfied."

3. "They utter insolent speech; all the workers of iniquity boast in themselves."

4. "The wicked glories in his greed. As for all his enemies, he sneers at them."[49]

+5. "His heart says, 'I shall never face adversity.'"

---

[48] *Sheol*
[49] *Gentleman*

6. "His mouth is full of cursing and oppression."

+7. "The men at peace with you shall deceive you and prevail against you. Your trusted friends have set a trap, but you are unaware."

8. "Do you indeed speak righteousness, you silent ones? Justice? You high and mighty politicians don't even know the meaning of the word. Fairness? Which of you has any left? Do you judge uprightly, you sons of men? No, in your heart you willingly commit crimes; on earth you look to the fruits of extortion."

9. "They proceed from evil to evil, and they do not know Me," says the LORD. "Everyone take heed to his neighbor, and do not trust your brothers. For every brother is a deceiver; every friend is guilty of slander. No one speaks the truth. They have taught their tongue to speak lies, and weary themselves to commit iniquity."

10. "Under his tongue are trouble and sin. He sits in the lurking places of[50] the villages. In the secret places he murders the innocent. His eyes are secretly fixed on the helpless. Like lions they crouch silently, waiting to pounce upon the poor. Like hunters they catch their victims in their traps."

11. "Their tongue is a deadly arrow. One speaks peaceably to his neighbor with his mouth, but inwardly he sets an ambush."

12. "Like a madman who throws firebrands, arrows, and death, is the man who deceives his neighbor, and says, 'I was only joking.'"

+13. "The words of his mouth are smoother than butter, but war is in his heart. His words are softer than oil, but they cut like sharp swords."

---

[50] Lurking

14.	"My soul is among lions who are set on fire, whose teeth are spears and arrows, and their tongues are daggers."
+15.	"Those who speak flattery to their friends and neighbors have evil in their hearts."[51]
+16.	"Deliver me and preserve me, O LORD, from evil and violent men, who abhor justice and twist all equity."
17.	"They sharpen their tongues like a serpent. The poison of asps is under their lips. They continually gather together for war, who plan evil things in their hearts."
18.	"Woe to those who scheme iniquity, who work out evil on their beds. When morning comes, they do it, for it is in the power of their hands."
19.	"They have closed up their fat hearts to pity. With their mouth they make exorbitant claims and proudly and arrogantly speak."
20.	Thus says the LORD, "Stand in the ways and see, and ask for the old paths, where the good way is, and walk in it. Then you will find rest for your souls. But they said, 'No, thanks.'"
21.	"This is the rest with which You may cause the weary to rest. This is the refreshing." Yet they would not hear.[52]
22.	"The whole vision has become to you like the words of a book that is sealed, which men deliver to one who is literate, saying, 'Read this, please'; and he says, 'I cannot, for it is sealed.' Then the book is delivered to one who is illiterate, saying, 'Read this, please'; and he says, 'I am not literate.'"

---

[51] *Pounce*
[52] *Exorbitant*

23. Then the LORD said, "This people draw near with their words and honor Me with their lip service, but they remove their hearts far from Me, and their reverence for Me consists of tradition learned by rote."

+24. They were disobedient and rebelled against YAH-way, and killed many of the prophets who had tried to give a warning in order to turn them back to the LORD.

25. "For he has crushed the poor and left them destitute."

+26. "It is ruthless men who retain their riches."

27. "A rich man will use you as long as he can profit from it, but when you need him, he will leave you helpless. If he needs you, he will trick you[53] with his smiles and cheerful, kindly words. 'Do you need anything?' he will ask. He will feed you until you are embarrassed. Finally, when he has drained you two or three times over, he will laugh at you. If you see him later, he will pretend he doesn't know you, and will pass you by."

28. "Though evil is sweet in his mouth, and he hides it under his tongue, yet his food in his stomach turns sour. It becomes cobra venom within him. He swallows down riches and vomits them up again. God casts them out of his belly."

29. "Deceitful scales are in his hand; he loves to oppress."

30. "A merchant can hardly avoid doing wrong. Every salesman is guilty of sin."

31. "It is hard to remove a peg that is stuck between two stones of a house, and it is just as hard to remove dishonesty from buying and selling."

---

[53]*Disobedient*

+32. "One who increases his possessions by usury and extortion, he who gives[54] gifts to the rich, and the wicked man who accepts a bribe, they all pervert the ways of justice."

33. "Are there not still treasures gained by wickedness in the house of the wicked? Is there to be no end of getting rich by cheating?"

34. "It isn't right for someone who is selfish to be rich. What use is money to a stingy person? If you deny yourself in order to accumulate wealth, you are only accumulating it for someone else. Others will use your riches to live in luxury. How can you be generous with others if you are stingy with yourself, if you are not willing to enjoy your own wealth? No one is worse off than someone who is stingy with himself; it is a sin that brings its own punishment. When such a person does something good, it is only by accident; his selfishness will sooner or later be evident. A selfish man is an evil man. He turns his back on people's needs and is never satisfied with what he has. Greed will shrivel up a person's soul."

+35. "If you shut your ears to the cry of the poor, you will also cry yourself and not be heard."[55]

36. "Behold, these are the ungodly, who are always at ease. They increase in riches, are settled in complacency, and say in their heart, 'The LORD will not do good, nor evil.'"

+37. There was one man, Moses, and his wife, Athaliah, who collected many of these teachings and placed them in a spot where the people could come to be inspired. They had the area fenced off and made into a shrine. It was called the Tabernacle of Witness. It became a substantial source of

---

[54] *Venom*
[55] *Accumulating*

income for him and her and their little ones.[56]

---

[56] *Athaliah*

Prophecy (Pr)

One--Haggai

1. Then Haggai, the LORD's messenger, spoke the LORD's message to the people.

2. "I am with you," says the LORD.

3. He read distinctly from the book, from the law of God, and he gave the sense, and helped them to understand the reading.

4. "All the men and women who could hear with understanding listened to me, and kept silence for my counsel. After my words they did not speak, and my speech settled on them as dew."

5. "Cry loudly, do not hold back. Raise your voice like a trumpet, and declare to My people their transgression, and to the house of Jacob their sins. Yet they seek Me day by day, and delight to know My ways, as a nation that has done righteousness, and has not forsaken the ordinance of their God. They ask Me for just decisions, and seem eager for My presence."[1]

6. "Why have we fasted," they say, "and You have not seen it? Why have we humbled ourselves, and You have not noticed?"

7. "When you fasted and mourned, did you really fast for Me--for Me? And when you were eating and drinking, were you not just feasting for yourselves?"

8. "In fact, in the day of your fast you find pleasure, and exploit all your laborers. Indeed, you fast for strife and debate, and to strike with the fist of

---

[1] *Haggai*

	wickedness."
9.	"And this is the second thing you do: you cover the altar of the LORD with tears, with weeping and crying. So He does not regard the offering anymore, nor receive it with good will from your hands."
10.	"Is it a fast like this which I choose, a day for a man to humble himself? Is it for bowing one's head like a reed, and for spreading out sackcloth and ashes as a bed?"
11.	"Is this not the fast which I choose: to loosen the bonds of wickedness,[2] to undo the heavy burdens, and to let the oppressed go free?"
+12.	"Is it not to share your bread with the hungry, and bring the homeless poor into your house, clothing the naked when you see them, and taking care of your own flesh?"
13.	"Then your light shall break forth like the morning, your healing shall spring forth speedily, the glory of the YAH-way shall be your rear guard, and your goodness will shield you. Then you shall call, and the LORD will answer. When you cry, He will say, 'Here I am.'"
14.	"Oh, that you had heeded My commandments! Then your peace would have been like a river, and your righteousness like the waves of the sea."
+15.	"The land is full of silver and gold and there is no end to its treasures. The land is also full of idols. You worship the work of your own hands, which your own fingers have made."
+16.	"A righteous person has this advantage over others: he or she does not[3] own any idols, so they haven't a chance to make him or her look foolish."

---

[2] *Loosen*
[3] *Advantage*

17.	"O Lord my God, my Holy One, You are forever righteous."
18.	"Both the inward thought and the heart of man are deep. The LORD is patient and will wait, that He may be gracious to you, for YAH-way is a God of justice."
19.	"All the saints of the Most High shall receive the kingdom."
+20.	"I will give you a new heart and put a new spirit within you. I will take out your hearts of stone and replace them with a heart of compassion. I will put My spirit within you, and you will no longer be reluctant to obey Me."
21.	"I will be your King."
+22.	"Believe in the LORD your God, and you shall be established. Believe the prophets of the YAH-way, and you shall prosper."[4]
23.	"Old men and old women will be sitting in the city squares. And the streets will again be full of boys and girls playing."
+24.	"Behold, I will bring health and healing, and reveal to them all an abundance of peace and truth."
25.	"In your midst I will leave a meek and humble people, who will come to Me for help. Nor shall a deceitful tongue be found in their mouth, and no one shall make them afraid."
+26.	"Who is the man that fears YAH-way? God will help him know which paths to choose. His soul shall dwell in goodness, and his descendants shall inherit the earth."

---

[4] *Patient*

27. "The sweet companionship and intimacy of the LORD is for those who revere and worship Him."

28. "In the days of famine they shall be satisfied."

29. "Oh, how great is Your goodness, which You have laid up for those who[5] fear You!"

30. "None of the wicked will have insight, but the wise shall understand."

31. "For I know the thoughts that I think toward you," says the LORD, "thoughts of peace and not of evil, to give you a future and a hope."

+32. "If you banish the yoke, the pointing of the finger, and speaking wickedness, if you extend your soul to the hungry and satisfy the needs of those around you, then your light will rise in darkness, and your gloom will become like midday."

33. "And the YAH-way will continually guide you, and satisfy your soul in scorched places, and strengthen your bones. You will be like a garden with a spring of water that never goes dry."

+34. "It is foolish to always trust in your own opinions. Whoever walks wisely (by following the teachings of wiser people) will be kept safe from many hardships."[6]

35. "The fear of man brings a snare, but whoever trusts in the YAH-way shall be secure."

+36. "Do not say 'a conspiracy,' concerning all that the people call a conspiracy, nor be afraid of their threats. But hallow and fear the LORD, and let God be your dread."

---

[5] *Boys*
[6] *Hardships*

37. "Many seek the ruler's favor, but the wise man waits for justice from the YAH-way."

38. "These commandments are not hidden nor too mysterious for you. It is not up in the sky. Nor is it across the sea, that you should say, 'Who will go across the ocean and bring it to us?' But the word is very near you, in your mouth and in your heart, that you may do it."

39. "See, I have set before you today life and good, death and evil. I have commanded you today to love the Lord your God and to follow his paths and to keep his laws, so that you will live and become a great nation, and so that the Lord your God will bless you."[7]

Two

+1. "If you will indeed obey My voice, then you shall be a special treasure to Me, and you shall be My kingdom of priests."

2. "Oh, that all the YAH-way's people were prophets and that the LORD would put His Spirit upon them!"

+3. "To whom will I teach knowledge? Who will understand the message? But these My people are like those just weaned from milk, like those recently drawn from the breasts. For precept must be upon precept, precept upon precept, line upon line, line upon line, here a little, there a little."

4. "But you, son of man, hear what I say to you. Do not be rebellious. Open your mouth and eat what I give you."

---

[7] *Mysterious*

5. "I will meditate with my heart, and my spirit ponders diligently."

6. "My soul, my whole heart, and my flesh cry out and thirst for God, the living God."[8]

7. "Show me Your ways, O YAH-way; teach me Your paths. Lead me in Your truth. For You are the God of my salvation. On You I wait all the day."

8. "Let the righteous strike me; it shall be a kindness. And let him reprove me, that I may walk before God in the light of the living."

+9. "I will answer your questions about My ways and teach you why the human race has an impulse to do evil."

10. "How sweet are Your words to my taste, sweeter than honey to my mouth! For You will light my lamp. The LORD my God, who is wonderful in counsel and excellent in guidance, will enlighten my darkness."

11. "I will stand my watch to see what the YAH-way will say to me, and what I will answer when I am reproved."

+12. "Fear not. You've done wickedly (for there is no one who does not sin), yet do not turn aside from following Me, but serve Me with all[9] your heart."

13. "And do not go after empty things which cannot profit or deliver, for they are nothing."

14. "For I looked, and there was no man; I looked among them, but there was no counselor, who, when asked, could answer a word. Indeed, their works are nothing,

---

[8] *Weaned*
[9] *Reprove*

	their molded images are wind and confusion."
15.	"What profit is the image, a teacher of lies, that its maker should carve it, that the maker of its mold should trust in it?"
16.	"Woe to him who says to wood, 'Awake!' To silent stone, 'Arise! It shall teach!' Behold, it is overlaid with gold and silver, and in it there is no breath at all."
+17.	"Every metalsmith is put to shame by the carved image, for his molded image is falsehood. They are futile, a work of errors. In the time of their punishment they shall perish. The Portion of Jacob is not like them, for I am the Maker of all things, and Israel is the tribe who has[10] inherited Me. The LORD of hosts is My name."
+18.	"I made the earth, and established the world through My understanding, and stretched out the heaven by My intuitive powers."
19.	"To whom will you liken Me, and make Me equal and compare Me, that we should be alike?"
+20.	"Be very careful. For you have spoken lies in My name and have not always spoken of Me what is true."
21.	"You have wearied Me with your words, in that you say, 'Everyone who does evil is good in the sight of God.'"
+22.	"Do you think this pleases Me?"
23.	"By a man of knowledge, right will be prolonged. But if you still do wickedly, you shall be swept away."
24.	"The lips of a priest should preserve knowledge, and people should seek[11] instruction from his mouth; for he is the messenger of the LORD of hosts."

---

[10] *Israel*
[11] *Inherited*

+25. "But he has departed from the way. He has caused many to stumble, and has corrupted the covenant of Levi."

26. "For they have committed fraud."

27. "They have lied about the YAH-way."

+28. "Ephraim has encompassed Me with lies, and the house of Israel has surrounded Me with misconstructions."

29. "Therefore preach against the holy places."

30. "Do not listen to the words of the prophets who prophesy to you, who make people stray, who chant 'Peace' when they have something to eat, but declare war against him who will not feed them, who swear by the name of the LORD, and make mention of the God of Israel, but not in truth or in righteousness. They fill you with emptiness and make you[12] worthless. They speak a vision of their own heart, not from the mouth of the LORD."

+31. "You live in a place with deceivers all around you."

32. "Heaping violence upon violence, and deceit upon deceit, they refuse to know Me," says the YAH-way."

33. "But there is a God in heaven who reveals secrets."

34. "According to the wisdom of the angel of God, we are able to know all things that are in the earth."

35. "Surely the Lord GOD does nothing unless He at least reveals His secrets to His servants the prophets."

36. "I have not spoken in secret, in a dark place of the earth. I did not say to the people of Israel, 'Seek Me in vain.' I am YAH-way, and I speak the truth; I make known what

---
[12] *Stray*

is right."[13]

37. "Hear, O My people, and I will admonish you! O Israel, if you will listen to Me!"

Three

1. "Son of man, your eyes shall see, and you shall say to all of your neighbors, 'Children oppress My people, and women rule over them. Those who lead you lead you astray, and destroy the way of your paths.'"

2. "Also say to them, 'I and the children whom the LORD has given me are for signs and wonders in Israel, from the LORD who dwells in Mount Zion. Incline your ears to the words of my mouth. I will speak in parables. I will utter dark sayings from of old, which our fathers have told us. I will not conceal the words of the Holy One.'"

3. "Tell them this as well, 'You also gave Your good Spirit to instruct them. For God may speak in one way, or in another. He who is blessed[14] in the earth shall be blessed by the God of truth, and he who swears in the earth shall swear by the God of truth. May the YAH-way destroy all flattering lips, and the tongue that speaks proud things.'"

4. My thoughts greatly alarmed me and my face grew pale. I was lying on my bed, troubled and disturbed.

5. I said to myself, "Some people are thought to be wise because they don't talk much; others are disliked because they talk too much."

---

[13] *Secrets*
[14] *Parables*

+6. But after taking counsel with myself further and emboldening my heart, I decided that I would make an accusation against the local nobles and ruling officials.

7. I said, "What you are doing is not good."

8. They were silent and could not find a word to say.

9. "Though you exalt yourself as high as the eagle, the pride of your heart has deceived you."[15]

+10. "You are men and not gods. And yet we are all aware of your pride and haughtiness. Your heart has become proud because of your riches."

+11. "I know your fury--an expression of your fear--but your boasts are false, and your lies and idle talk have made nothing right."

12. "By the abundance of your trading you became filled with violence within, and you sinned against your soul."

13. "You have said, 'I am perfect in beauty.'"

14. "Behold, I am against you, O you most proud!" says the Lord GOD of hosts.

+15. "A lovely woman who lacks discretion is like a ring of gold in a swine's snout. So also is a rich person who has no gratitude or humility."

+16. "He speaks pompous words against the Most High. He consults a medium for guidance, but does not inquire of the YAH-way. He persecutes the saints of the Highest One, and intends to make[16] alterations in times and in law, for a time and times and half a

---

[15] *Alarmed*
[16] *Haughtiness*

	time."
17.	Thus says the Redeemer, "You have been weighed in the balances, and found wanting."
18.	"I am YAH-way, who formed you from the womb, who makes all things, who stretches out the heavens, who spreads abroad the earth, who frustrates the signs of the babblers, who overthrows the learning of the wise and turns it into nonsense."
+19.	"From the place of God's habitation, all of the inhabitants of the earth are seen. The YAH-way fashions their hearts individually, considers all their works, and gives to everyone according to each of their ways."
+20.	"For You, only You, know the hearts of all earth's sons and daughters."
21.	"O Jerusalem, wash your heart from wickedness, that you may be saved. How long shall your evil thoughts lodge within you?"
22.	Yet they would not listen. They mocked God's messengers, despised[17] their words, and scoffed at the prophets until there was no longer any remedy against the anger of the Lord.
23.	"Listen carefully to my speech. Bear with me that I may speak, and after I have spoken, keep mocking. Be quiet. Let me speak, then come what may!"
24.	"Many shall run to and fro, and knowledge shall increase. Everyone's heart is as hard as stone, for your iniquity teaches your mouth, and you choose the tongue of the crafty. Your own mouth condemns you, and not I."
25.	"Let the wicked fall into their own nets, for there is none among them who calls upon Me."

---

[17] Babblers

26.	"And the people will oppress one another. Everyone will take advantage of everyone."
+27.	"When a wicked dastard arises in power, a prudent person foresees the evil and hides himself."[18]
28.	"Confidence in an unfaithful man in times of trouble is like a bad tooth or a foot out of joint. It is better to trust in the LORD than to put confidence in man. It is better to trust in the LORD than to put confidence in princes."
29.	"Sing O barren, you who have not borne! Break forth into singing, and cry aloud, you who have not travailed with child! For more are the children of the desolate than the children of the married woman," says the YAH-way.
30.	"Woe to those who justify the wicked for a bribe, and take away justice from the righteous man!"
+31.	"Now shall be their perplexity. They will throw their wealth into the streets, and their gold will be of no use and will not be able to deliver them. When each of them comes to his end, none shall help him. Their souls will not be satisfied and their stomachs will be empty. Their silver and their gold became their stumbling block of iniquity."
32.	"Understand, son of man. Prepare yourself and be ready. Arise, go up[19] to the wealthy nation that dwells securely," says the LORD, "which has neither gates nor bars, dwelling alone. Do not be afraid of their words or dismayed by their looks."
33.	"O my soul, my soul! I am pained in my very heart! My heart makes a noise in me. I cannot hold my peace. I am weary of holding it in."

---

[18] *Dastard*
[19] *Travailed*

34. "To whom shall I speak and give warning, that they may hear? Indeed their ear is uncircumcised, and they cannot give heed. Behold, the word of God is a reproach to them; they have no delight in it."

35. "I will be pleased with the few who will be saved, because they are the ones who now praise and honor Me and make My name known. I will not be sad about the large number of people who will be lost, because even now they last no longer than a vapor. They disappear like fire and smoke. They catch fire, blaze up, and quickly go out."

36. "Sigh therefore, son of man, with a breaking heart, and sigh with bitterness before their eyes. And it shall be when they say to you, 'Why are you sighing?' that you shall answer, 'Because there are those[20] who rebel against the light. They do not know its ways nor abide in its paths. They pervert the way of the humble."

37. And I said, "Oh, that I had wings like a dove! For then I would fly away and be at rest. For I have seen violence and strife in the city; deceit and guile do not depart from its streets."

38. "They were unfaithful to Me, when they dwelt safely in their own land and no one made them afraid."

39. "When they had pasture, they were filled. They were filled and their heart was exalted. Therefore, they forgot Me. Now they sin more and more."

Four

1. "A son honors his father, and a servant his master. If

---

[20] *Uncircumcised*

then I am the Father, where is My honor? And if I am a Master, where is My²¹ reverence?" says YAH-way.

2. "In what way have we despised Your name?"

+3. "You did not walk according to the ways of those who preceded you, but, as if their transgressions were too tame for you, you became even more corrupt than they were."

4. "You erected your shrine at the head of every road. Yet you were not like a harlot, because you scorned payment. You are an adulterous wife, who takes strangers instead of her husband. Men make payment to all harlots, but you made your payments to all your lovers, and hired them to come to you from all around. You are the opposite of other women, because no one solicited you."

5. "How degenerate is your heart!" says the Lord GOD, "seeing you do all these things, the deeds of a brazen harlot."

6. "I hate, I despise your feast days, and I do not savor your sacred assemblies. Take away from Me the noise of your songs, for I will not²² hear the melody of your stringed instruments. I will not accept them."

7. "The YAH-way hates the gifts of the wicked, but loves those who follow and pursue righteousness."

8. "Reform your ways and your actions. Turn back from your evil paths. Make your deeds good."

9. But they replied, "That is hopeless! Don't waste your breath. We have no intention of doing what God says. We will continue to live as we want to, free from any restraint."

---

²¹ *Land*
²² *Degenerate*

10. "Now go, write it on a tablet, and note it on a scroll, that it may be for time to come, forever and ever, that this is a rebellious people, lying children, children who will not hear the law of the YAH-way, who say to the seers, 'Do not see,' and to the prophets, 'Do not prophesy to us right things. Speak to us smooth things. Tell us nice things. Tell us what we want to hear. Let us keep our illusions. Don't tell us the truth. Get out of the way. Turn aside from the path. Cause the Holy One to cease from before us.'"[23]

11. Thus says the Holy One of Israel: "Because you despise this word, and trust in oppression, and rely on perversity, you will be shattered like the breaking of the potter's vessel, which is broken in pieces, whose breaking comes suddenly, in an instant."

+12. "Why then has this people slidden back in a perpetual backsliding? They hold fast to deceit; they do not speak aright. No one repents of his or her deplorable conduct, but says, 'What have I done?' Each one turns to pursue his own ends."

13. "Why? Because I have seen a horrible thing in the prophets of Jerusalem: they commit adultery and walk in lies. They also strengthen the hands of evildoers, so that no one turns back from his wickedness."

14. "How shall I pardon you? Shall I count pure those with the wicked balances, and with the bag of deceitful weights? Your children have forsaken Me and sworn by those that are not gods. When I had fed them to the full, then they committed adultery and assembled themselves by troops in the harlots' houses."[24]

15. "They were like well-fed lusty stallions. Every one neighed after his neighbor's wife. The unfaithful are

---

[23] *Hopeless*
[24] *Perversity*

	trapped by their own lust. Shall I not punish them for these things?" says YAH-way. "And shall I not avenge Myself on such a nation as this?"
16.	"Woe to those who drag iniquity with cords of falsehood, and sin as if with a cart rope, by feasting on the poor in secret."
17.	"For My people are foolish; they have not known Me. They are silly children, and they have no understanding. They are wise to do evil, but to do good they have no knowledge."
18.	"They are all estranged from Me by their false gods."
+19.	"The hope of ungrateful people melts away like a wintry frost, and runs off like wasted water."
20.	"I was crushed by their adulterous heart which has departed from Me, and by their eyes which play the prostitute after their idols."[25]
21.	"Woe to him who covets evil gain for his house, that he may set his nest on high."
22.	"I beat My fists at the dishonest profit which you have made."
23.	"All of you are liars, each man and each woman in the entire multitude of Israel."
24.	"Your injury has no healing, your wound is severe. For upon whom has not your wickedness passed continually?"
25.	"Is it not evil? Is it not evil?"
26.	"They did not cry out to Me with their heart when they wailed upon their beds."

---

[25] *Avenge*

27. "And the land shall mourn, every family by itself."

28. "Much pain is in every side, nor shall their sacrifices be pleasing to Him."[26]

+29. "Because you do not take it to heart, but have rebelled against and grieved the YAH-way's Holy Spirit."

30. "What you have in your mind shall never be, when you say, 'We will be like the Gentiles, like the families in other countries, serving wood and stone.'"

31. "They lavish gold out of the bag, and weigh silver in the balance. They hire a goldsmith, and he makes it a god. They prostrate themselves; yes, they worship. Though one cries out to it, yet it cannot answer nor save him out of his trouble."

+32. "From their silver and gold they make idols for themselves--but a workman has made it, and it is not God!"

33. But they would not listen. They refused to heed, shrugged their shoulders, and stopped their ears so that they could not hear. And they made their hearts as hard as flint."

34. "Oh, that my head were waters, and my eyes a fountain of tears, that I[27] might weep day and night, that I might leave my people, and go from them! For they are all adulterers, an assembly of treacherous men. And like their bow they have bent their tongue for lies. They are not valiant for the truth on the earth."

35. "They do not know the thoughts of the YAH-way, nor do they understand His counsel."

---

[26] *Wailed*
[27] *Flint*

+36.   "Do horses run on rocks? Can you plow the sea with oxen? Yet you have not labored for justice but have turned it into wormwood. You have not grown the fruit of righteousness into your lives but instead bitterness and poison, and have killed the concept of uprightness, because you trample upon the poor."

37.   "Woe to him who builds a town with bloodshed, who establishes a city by iniquity!"

38. Through his cunning he shall cause deceit to prosper, and he shall magnify himself in his heart.[28]

+39. He shall cast truth down to the ground. But he did all this and still prospered.

40. And he sacrificed one of his sons as a burnt offering on a heathen altar. He practiced black magic and consulted fortunetellers and wizards.

41. So YAH-way was very angry.

42.   "For your iniquities you have sold yourselves."

+43.   "But You were to them the God-Who-Forgives."

44. "You looked for much, but indeed it came to little; and when you brought it home, I blew it away. Why?" says the LORD of hosts. "Because of My house, which remains a ruin, while each of you is busy with his own house."

+45. "Coastlands, listen to Me in silence. You have spent your strength for nothing and in vain. Let us come together for judgment. Let them approach, then let them speak. And let the peoples gain new strength."[29]

---

[28] *Bloodshed*
[29] *Coastlands*

Five

1. "Now therefore," thus says the YAH-way: "Consider your ways! You have sown much, and bring in little; you eat, but do not have enough; you drink, but you are not filled; you clothe yourselves, but no one is warm. And he who earns wages, earns wages to put into a bag with holes." Thus says the Lord of hosts: "Consider your conduct and how you have fared."

2. "You have sold yourselves for nothing, and you shall be redeemed without money."

3. Then I prayed, "O Lord above, permit me, your humble servant, to offer this prayer: Plant a seed within us, and let it grow until it produces new hearts and minds, so that sinful humanity may have life. For you alone are God, and you created all of us. You give life and provide arms and legs to the body formed in the womb, where it is kept safe and carried for nine months. Then when the womb delivers what was created in it, your command produces milk from the breasts of the human body."[30]

4. "Righteous are You, O YAH-way, when I plead with You; yet let me talk with You about Your justice. Why does the way of the wicked prosper? Why are those happy who deal so treacherously? You have planted them, yes, they have taken root. They grow, yes, they bear fruit. You are near in their mouth but far from their mind."

5. "You our God have punished us less than our iniquities deserve."

6. "Our iniquities have risen higher than our heads, yet God does not charge them with wrongdoing."

---

[30] *Holes*

+7.	"Could the YAH-way in fact and reality be merciful and gracious, and slow to anger and abounding in forgiveness?"
+8.	"Will God not render to each person according to their deeds?"
9.	"I, the LORD, search the heart, I test the mind, to give each person according to the way he lives, and according to the fruit of his doings."
10.	"There is emptiness for the empty and fullness for the full."[31]
11.	"Let, I pray, Your merciful kindness be for my comfort."
12.	"Listen to the cry and to the prayer which Thy servant prays before Thee."
13.	"My harp is turned to mourning, and my flute to the sound of those who weep, for those whom I love have turned against me."
14.	"They gape at me with their mouth, they strike me reproachfully on the cheek, they gather together against me."
15.	"I am the just and blameless who is laughed to scorn."
16.	"Where shall I seek comforters?"
17.	"For there is no one who acknowledges me; no one cares for my soul."
18.	"Revive me according to Your lovingkindness."
19.	"For my life is spent with grief, and my years with

---

[31] *Treacherously*

sighing."[32]

20. "My sighing is not hidden from You. My heart pants, my strength fails me. As for the light of my eyes, it also has gone from me. My loved ones and my friends stand aloof."

21. "I am so troubled that I cannot speak."

22. "I have proclaimed the good news of righteousness. I have not concealed Your lovingkindness and Your truth from the great congregation. I have not hidden Your righteousness within my heart."

23. "Uphold me with Your generous Spirit."

24. "Surely I will not go into the chamber of my house, or go up to the comfort of my bed. I will not give sleep to my eyes or slumber to my eyelids."

25. He ate no bread and drank no water, and he also stripped off his clothes and lay down naked all that day and all that night.

+26. "Did I not fear You and seek YAH-way's favor? But I am a worm, and[33] not a man; a reproach of men, and despised by the people. All those who see me laugh at me. They hurl insults, they stick out their tongues and shake their heads."

27. "You relied on YAH-way," they say. "Why doesn't he save you? If the LORD likes you, why doesn't he help you?"

+28. "I am Your servant; help me to comprehend."

29. "Why is my pain perpetual and my wound incurable, which refuses to be healed? Wilt thou indeed be to me like a deceptive stream, with water that is unreliable?"

---
[32] *Acknowledges*
[33] *Stripped*

30.	"Your words were found, and I ate them, and Your word was to me the joy and rejoicing of my heart. I sat alone because of Your hand, for You have filled me with indignation."
+31.	"For Your sake I have been taunted, because zeal for the YAH-way has eaten me up."[34]
32.	"Cursed be the day in which I was born! Let the day not be blessed in which my mother bore me! Let the man be cursed who brought news to my father, saying, 'A male child has been born to you!' making him very glad. And let that man be like the cities which the LORD overthrew, and did not relent. Let him hear the cry in the morning and the shouting at noon, because he did not kill me from the womb, that my mother might have been my grave."
33.	"Why did I come forth from the womb to see labor and sorrow, that my days should be consumed with shame?"
34.	"Why then have You brought me out of the womb? Oh, that I had perished and no eye had seen me! I would have been as though I had not been. I would have been carried from the womb to the grave."
35.	"Are not my days few? Cease! Leave me alone, that I may take a little comfort before I go to the place from which I shall not return, to the land of darkness and the shadow of death; a land as dark as darkness itself, as the shadow of death, without any order, where even the light is like darkness."[35]
36.	"Woe is me, my mother, that you have borne me, a man of strife and a man of contention to the whole earth! I have neither lent for interest, nor have men lent to me for interest. Every one of them curses

---

[34] *Hurl*
[35] *Shouting*

	me."
+37.	"Why should I go on living?"
38.	"I will speak, that I may find relief; I must open my lips. Let me not, I pray, show partiality to anyone. Nor let me flatter any man, for I do not know how to flatter."
39.	"I am full of words. The spirit within me compels me. Indeed, my bosom is like wine that has no vent. It is ready to burst like new wineskins."
40.	"Look down from heaven, and see from Your habitation, holy and glorious. Where are Your zeal and Your strength, the yearning of Your heart and Your mercies toward me? Are they restrained?"
41.	"Doubtless You are our Father, O YAH-way. Our Redeemer from Everlasting is Your name."[36]
42.	"O God, why have You made us stray from Your ways, and hardened our hearts?"
43.	"Neither our kings nor our princes, our priests nor our fathers, have kept Your law, nor heeded Your commandments."
44.	"Surely joy has withered away from the sons of men."
+45.	"Who can understand his errors? Cleanse me from secret faults. Refrain Your servant also from presumptuous sins. Let them not have dominion over me. Then I shall be blameless."
46.	"Why is your spirit so sullen?"
47.	"I have heard your prayer. I have seen your tears. Surely I will heal you."

---

[36] *Why*

48. "They have not rejected you, but they have rejected Me, that I should not reign over them."[37]

49. "Son of man, your fellow citizens who talk about you by the walls and in the doorways of the houses, speak to one another, saying, 'Come now, and hear what the message is which comes forth from the YAH-way.' And they come to you: 'Please inquire for the word of the LORD today.' And they sit before you as My people, and they hear what you say but they will not do it."

+50. "For their lips speak insincerity to fulfill their lustful desires, and their heart is fixed in the pursuit of profit."

51. "Indeed you are to them as a very lovely love song of one who has a pleasant voice and can play well on an instrument. To them you are nothing more than an entertainer. For they hear your words, but they do not do them."

52. "I say unto them: Behold, I am weighed down by you, as a wagon totters when filled with grain; for the sin of their mouth and the words of their lips, and for the cursing and lying which they speak."

53. "Alas, you who are longing for the day of the LORD. For what purpose[38] will the day be to you? It will be darkness and not light; as when a man flees from a lion, and a bear meets him, or went into the house and leaned with his hand against the wall, and a serpent bit him."

+54. "Yes, gather yourselves together, O shameless nation. Seek the YAH-way, with the prudent people of the earth, who have upheld God's commands. Seek righteousness. Seek humility."

55. "My heart churns within Me. My sympathy is stirred,

---

[37] *Presumptuous*
[38] *Entertainer*

	son of man, because your heart was tender, and you humbled yourself."
56.	"But I will correct you in justice, and will not let you go altogether unpunished."
+57.	"I have given the earth to the children of men."
58.	"Ask the earth. Let her tell you that she is the one who ought to be mourning for the vast multitudes of people that she has brought to birth. All of us who are living came originally from her, and there are more to come. Almost all of us go straight to destruction--the vast[39] multitude of earth's children are lost."
+59.	"So who has more of a right to mourn: you, or the earth which has such sadness?"
60.	"O Lord, forgive!"
61.	"We come to You with repentant hearts and humble spirits."
62.	"Turn us back to You, O YAH-way, unless You have utterly rejected us."
+63.	"When we return to You with all our heart and with all our soul, rain down from above, and let the skies pour out Your pure rectitude upon us."
+64.	"Do you hope for My mercy and loving-kindness? You shall have it--I, the YAH-way, have created it!"[40]

---

[39]*Serpent*
[40]*Repentant*

Six--Habakkuk....

1. The burden which the prophet Habakkuk saw--Violence!

2. "Heed the voice of the words of YAH-way."

3. "Woe to those who accumulate houses, who add field to field."

+4. The more possessions people gather, the more they spend on their cities and houses, the more attention they give to their personal appearance, the more angry YAH-way becomes because of their sin.

5. "The plunder of the poor is in your houses. What do you mean by crushing My people and grinding the faces of the poor?"

6. The YAH-way my God said to me, "Feed the flock doomed for slaughter. Those who buy them slay them and go unpunished, and each of those who sells them says, 'Blessed be the YAH-way, for I have become rich!' And their own shepherds have no pity on them."

7. "I will no longer have pity on the inhabitants of this land," says[41] YAH-way. "I will cause men to fall each into the hand of his shepherd, and each into the hand of his king. And they shall crush the earth, and I will deliver none from their hand."

8. So I fed the flock, in particular the poor of the flock. I took for myself two staffs: the one I called Beauty, and the other I called Bonds. And I fed the flock as I had been told to do.

9. I dismissed three shepherds in one month. My soul loathed them. But the flock detested me, and I grew weary of them.

---

[41] *Slaughter*

10.	Then I said, "I will not feed you. Let what is dying die, and what is perishing perish. Let those that are left eat each other's flesh."
11.	And I took my staff, Beauty, and cut it in two, that I might break the covenant which I had made with all the peoples. So it was broken on that day. Thus the poor of the flock, who were watching me, knew that the YAH-way was speaking through what I did.
12.	Then I said to them, "If it is agreeable to you, give me my wages, and if[42] not, refrain."
13.	So they weighed out for my wages thirty pieces of silver.
14.	And YAH-way said to me, "Throw it to the potter"--that princely price they thought I was worth.
15.	So I took the thirty pieces of silver and threw them into the house of the LORD for the potter.
16.	Then I cut in two my other staff, Bonds, that I might break the brotherhood between Judah and Israel.
17.	And YAH-way said to me, "Next, take for yourself the implements of a foolish shepherd. For behold, I am going to raise up a shepherd in the land who will not care for the perishing, seek the scattered, heal the broken, or nourish the healthy, but will eat the meat of the choice sheep and tear their hooves in pieces."
18.	"Woe to the worthless shepherd who doesn't care for the flock. He has[43] abandoned them."
19.	"Why should I fear in the days of evil, when the iniquity at my heels surrounds me? Those who trust in their wealth and boast in the multitude of their riches, none of them can by any means redeem his

---

[42] *Dismissed*
[43] *Nourish*

	brother, nor give to God a ransom."
+20.	"O God, why have You made men like the fish of the sea, like creeping things without a ruler over them? The misleading prophets bring all of them up with a hook, drag them away with their net, and gather them together in their fishing net. Therefore, they rejoice and are glad."
21.	"They offer a sacrifice to their net, and burn incense, because by these things their share is sumptuous, and their food is plentiful."
22.	"In all our farming communities are those who go up on the roof and who worship the sun, moon, and stars on the housetops."
+23.	"They are those who formerly worshiped the YAH-way, but now serve and swear by the name of the Ammonite god called Molech. They also[44] marry the daughters of other strange gods. These have fallen away from YAH-way, and have stopped inquiring of Him."
24.	"Multitudes, multitudes in the valley of decision!"
25.	"I have loved you," YAH-way says.
26.	Yet you say, "In what way have You loved us?"
+27.	"Jacob and Israel, why do you say, 'My way is hidden from God, and my just claims have been ignored by the LORD?'"
+28.	"Have you not known? Have you not heard? YAH-way is the eternal God. The Creator of the ends of the earth neither faints nor is weary. His wisdom is inexhaustible. He gives power to the weak, and to those who have no might He increases

---

[44] *Hook*

strength."

29. "Even the youths shall faint and be weary, and the young men shall stumble badly. Yet those who hope in the YAH-way will gain new strength. They will sprout wings like eagles. They will soar and not[45] grow weary; they will walk and not become faint."

30. He knelt down on his knees three times that day, and prayed and gave thanks before his God, as was his custom.

+31. "But I am poor and sorrowful. For the redemption of their souls is costly: so that they may live in eternity, and not be spoiled by corruption."

+32. "Buck up. Keep at it. My Spirit shall not abide with a man forever. Your days shall be no more than one hundred and twenty years."

+33. "Put a mark on the forehead of a man who sighs and cries."

34. "Behold, My Servant shall deal prudently. He shall be raised high and greatly exalted. Just as many were astonished at you, so His visage was marred more than any man, and His form more than the sons of men. So shall He startle many nations. Kings shall shut their mouths at Him. For what had not been told them they shall see, and what they had not heard they shall consider."[46]

35. "But, oh, how few believe it! Who will listen? To whom will God reveal his saving power? For He shall grow up as a tender plant, and as a root out of dry ground. He has no stately form or comeliness. And when we see Him, there is no beauty that we should desire Him. He is despised and rejected by men, a Man of sorrows and acquainted with grief. And we hid, as it were, our faces from Him. He was despised, and we did not esteem

---

[45] *Inexhaustible*
[46] *Startle*

Him. We ignored Him as if He were nothing."

36. "Surely He has borne our sicknesses and carried our pains. Yet we reckoned Him stricken by God, and afflicted. But He was wounded for our transgressions. He was bruised for our iniquities. The chastisement for our peace was upon Him, and by the blows He received we are healed."

37. "All we like sheep have gone astray. We have turned, every one, to his own way. And YAH-way has laid on Him the iniquity of us all."

38. "He was oppressed and harshly treated, yet He opened not His mouth. He was led as a lamb to the slaughter. As a sheep before its shearers is silent, so also He did not open His mouth."[47]

39. "He was taken from prison and from judgment, and who will declare His generation? For He was cut off from the land of the living for the sin of My people. And they made His grave with the wicked and with a rich man at His death."

40. "Though He had done no wrong nor spoken any falsehood, yet it pleased the YAH-way to crush Him."

+41. "When You make His soul an offering for sin, You get to see Your seed prolonged. God shall see the toil of His soul, and be satisfied."

42. "By His knowledge My righteous Servant shall justify many, for He shall bear their iniquities. Therefore, I will divide Him a portion with the great, because He poured out His life unto death."

+43. "He was treated as a sinner, but has interceded on their behalf."

---

[47] *Reckoned*

+44. "Having in His hand a drawn sword, the LORD commanded Him to return His sword to its sheath."[48]

45. "The Messiah shall suffer the death penalty, but not for Himself."

46. "The stone will cry out from the wall, and the beam from the rafters will answer it."

47. "The stone which the builders rejected has become the chief cornerstone. This was done by the YAH-way."

48. "Turn back, O virgin of Israel. How long will you gad about, O you backsliding daughter? For the YAH-way has created a new thing--a woman shall encompass a man."

49. And in that day seven women shall take hold of one man, saying, "Behold, I was brought forth in iniquity, and in sin my mother conceived me. We will eat our own food and wear our own apparel. Only let us be called by your name, to take away our disgrace."

50. "Has it not been told you from the beginning? Have you not understood from the foundations of the earth? It is He who sits above the circle of the earth, and its inhabitants are like grasshoppers, who[49] stretches out the heavens like a curtain, and spreads them out like a tent to dwell in. He reduces the princes to nothing. He makes the judges of the earth useless."

51. "Surely all the inhabitants of the earth are reputed as nothing. He does according to His will in heaven and among the inhabitants of the earth. No one can

---

[48] *Interceded*
[49] *Grasshoppers*

restrain His hand or say to Him, 'What have You done?'"

52. Thus says YAH-way: "Cursed is the man who trusts in man and makes flesh his strength, whose heart departs from Me. For he shall be like a shrub in the desert, and shall not see good when it comes."

+53. "Please let me fall into Your merciful hands, but do not let me fall into the hands of man."

54. "For You, my God, are good, and ready to forgive, and abundant in mercy to all those who call upon You."

55. "How precious also are Your thoughts to me, O God! How great is the sum of them! If I should count them, they would be more in number[50] than the sand. When I awake, I am still with You."

56. "He reveals deep and secret things, He knows what is in the darkness, and light dwells with Him."

57. "YAH-way preserves the simple. I was brought low,

---

[50] *Shrub*

	and He saved me. Return to your rest, O my soul, for the YAH-way has dealt bountifully with you."
58.	"Come and hear, all you who fear God, and I will declare what He has done for my soul."
59.	"Turn to Him with all your heart and soul. Live in loyal obedience to Him. Then He will turn to you to help you and will no longer hide Himself. Remember what God has done for you, and give thanks with all your heart. Praise the righteous Lord; honor the eternal King. Although I live in exile in a foreign land, I will give thanks to the YAH-way and will speak of His great strength to a nation of sinners. Turn away from your sins, and do what pleases God! Perhaps He will be gracious and show you His mercy."[51]
60.	"Trust YAH-way, and He will help you. Walk straight in His ways, and put your hope in Him."
+61.	"If you refuse to accept correction, you are committing a sin. But if you venerate the YAH-way, you will make a sincere change in your ways."
62.	"He will guard the feet of His saints."
63.	"The YAH-way is good, a stronghold in the day of trouble, and He knows those who trust in Him."
64.	"But can anyone be righteous in the eyes of God?"
65.	"Where is the God of justice?"
66.	"What confidence is this in which you trust?"
67.	"Go out, and stand on the mountain before

---

[51] *Turn*

YAH-way."[52]

68. And behold, the YAH-way passed by, and a great and strong wind tore into the mountains and broke the rocks in pieces, but the YAH-way was not in the wind. And after the wind an earthquake, but the YAH-way was not in the earthquake. And after the earthquake a fire, but YAH-way was not in the fire.

+69. "I have sent to you all My servants the prophets, sending them again and again, saying: 'Turn now every one of you from wicked ways, and be straight in your behavior, and do not go after other gods to serve them.'"

70. "Defend the poor and fatherless. Do justice, and you will seek Me and find Me, when you search for Me with all your heart."

+71. "I will forgive your iniquities when you turn from your harmful way."[53]

Seven

1. "YAH-way created human beings and gave each one of them a heart. He gave them life, breath, and understanding, which is the spirit of God."

2. "Do not be like the horse or like the mule, which have no understanding, which must be harnessed with bit and bridle, else they will not come near you."

3. "Lift up your eyes to the heavens, and look on the earth beneath. For the heavens will vanish away like smoke, the earth will grow old like a garment, and those who

---

[52] *Straight*
[53] *Harmful*

dwell in it will die in like manner, but My salvation will be forever, and My righteousness will not be abolished."

4. To him who is without sense She says, "Whoever is simple and thoughtless, let him turn in here! Come, eat of My bread and drink of the wine which I have mixed. Forsake foolishness and live, and go in the way of understanding."

5. "Since the Lord's spirit fills the entire world, and holds everything in it[54] together, She knows every word that people say."

6. "Wisdom is a spirit that is friendly to people, but She will not forgive anyone who speaks against God, because God is the witness of our feelings and thoughts, and the sure observer of our every word."

7. "Am I a God near at hand," says the YAH-way, "and not a God far away? Can anyone hide himself in secret places, so I shall not see him? Do I not fill heaven and earth?"

8. "It shall come to pass that before they call, I will answer, and while they are still speaking, I will hear."

9. "Surely in YAH-way I have righteousness and strength. To Him men shall come, and all shall be ashamed who are incensed against Him."

10. "Woe to the rebellious children who take counsel, but not of Me, and who devise plans, but not of My Spirit."

11. "Who may dwell in Your holy hill? He whose walk is blameless and[55] who does what is righteous, who speaks the truth from his heart and does not backbite with his tongue, who does no evil to his friend and harms not his fellow man."

---

[54] *Abolished*
[55] *Ashamed*

12. "He who does these things shall never be moved, and this One shall be peace."

13. "How beautiful upon the mountains are the feet of him who brings good news, who proclaims peace, who brings glad tidings of good things, who proclaims salvation."

14. "In Your majesty ride prosperously because of truth, humility, and righteousness."

15. "Bind up the testimony, seal the law among my disciples."

16. "The tongue of the wise uses knowledge rightly. To the law and to the testimony! If they do not speak according to this word, it is because there is no light in them."[56]

17. "And they will pass through it hard pressed and hungry. And it shall happen, when they are hungry, that they will be enraged and curse their king and their God, and look upward. Then they will look to the earth, and see trouble and darkness, gloom of anguish, and they will be thrust into thick darkness."

+18. "Where there is no widespread revelation, the people become demoralized and cast off all restraint. But blessed is he who keeps the law."

19. The word of the YAH-way also came to me, saying, "You shall not take a wife, nor shall you have sons or daughters in this place."

+20. "Maintain your integrity. Do not incite Me to ruin you against My will."

21. "After my skin is destroyed, this I know, that in my

---

[56] Backbite

flesh I shall see God."

22. "It is better to dwell in the wilderness than with a contentious and[57] angry woman; it is better to dwell in a corner of a housetop than in a house shared with a nagging, quarrelsome and faultfinding woman."

23. The word of YAH-way came to me again saying, "Son of man, it is better to go to your grave with no children at all than to have children who are godless."

24. "I was sought by those who did not ask for Me; I was found by those who did not seek Me. I said, 'Here I am, here I am,' to a nation that was not called by My name."

25. "I will take the dazzling light of My presence away from Israel, and will give to My new people the eternal Temple that I had prepared for Israel. I give My solemn promise that I will bless those people, and deep within them they will believe My words."

26. "I have stretched out My hands all day long to a rebellious people, who walk in a way that is not good, according to their own thoughts; a people who continually provoke Me to My face."[58]

27. "Go by day in their sight, for perhaps even yet they will consider Me again."

28. "And the Sun of Righteousness shall arise with healing in His wings. The Lord GOD will wipe away tears from all faces. He shall speak peace to the nations."

29. "I will heal their backsliding. I will love them freely."

30. "Be on the earth, on the face of the whole earth, for mercy."

---

[57] *Hungry*
[58] *Housetop*

31.		"A scepter of righteousness is the scepter of Your kingdom."
+32.		"The heavens declare the glory of God, and the firmament shows Your handiwork. Day unto day utters speech, and night unto night reveals knowledge. There is no speech nor language where their voice is not heard. Their line has gone out through all the earth, and their words to the end of the world, that all people of the earth may know Your name and fear You."[59]
33.		"See, the former things have taken place, and new things I declare; before they spring into being I announce them to you."
34.		"Come here, and I will light the lamp of understanding in your heart, and it will not go out until you have finished what you are supposed to write. When you have finished your work, you will make some of it public, and you will give the rest to wise men, who will keep it secret."
35.		"My heart is overflowing with a good theme. I recite my composition concerning the King. My tongue is the pen of a ready writer."
36.		"Take heed, all you people!"
37.		"Behold, a king will reign in righteousness, and princes will rule with justice."
38.		"His name shall be Peaceful; a man of rest. In his days there will be peace and quietness."
39.		"A man will be as a hiding place from the wind, and a cover from the[60] tempest, as rivers of water in a dry

---

[59] *Handiwork*
[60] *Overflowing*

	place, as the shadow of a great rock in a weary land. The eyes of those who see will not be dim, and the ears of those who hear will listen."
40.	"Also the heart of the hasty will understand knowledge, and the tongue of the stammerers will be ready to speak plainly."
41.	"Every man will go to his place of possession."
42.	"Everyone shall sit under his vine and under his fig tree, and no one shall make them afraid, that they may see and know, and consider and understand together, that the hand of the YAH-way has done this, and the Holy One of Israel has created it."
+43.	"YAH-way will be called the God of the whole earth, and His house shall be called a house of prayer for all nations."
44.	"Shall He who shaped the ear not hear? or He who formed the eye not see?"[61]
+45.	"He who instructs the nations, He who teaches man knowledge, shall He not also correct us when we err?"
46.	"Ask Me of things to come concerning My sons, and concerning the work of My hands. I have made the earth, and created human beings on it. It was I--My hands that stretched out the heavens, and all their host I have commanded."
+47.	"I have raised them up in righteousness, and I will make all their ways straight. They shall build My city and let My exiles go free, not for price nor reward," says the YAH-way.

---

[61] *Fig*

Eight

1. "O Lord, you created me, and I am your servant, so listen to my prayer. As long as I have life and understanding, I cannot keep silent."

2. "What good is it to us that we have the promise of immortal life, when[62] we have committed sins that condemn us to death? What good is it that Paradise is shown to us, that its imperishable fruit can heal us and provide all we need? We can never go there because we have lived unacceptable lives."

3. Then the YAH-way answered and said, "Write the vision and make it plain on tablets, that the one who reads it may run and fly toward the goal."

4. "YAH-way is gracious and full of compassion. He will teach us His ways, and we shall walk in His paths. And He shall stand and feed His flock until the Spirit is poured upon us."

5. "And it shall be in that day that you will call Me 'my Husband,' and no longer call Me 'my Master.'"

6. "In that day I will make a covenant for them with the beasts of the field, with the birds of the air, and with the creeping things of the ground. There shall be no more war; bow and sword of battle I will shatter from the earth, to make them lie down safely in a peaceful[63] habitation, in secure dwellings, and in quiet resting places, as it was long ago in Eden, the garden of God."

7. "Then justice will dwell in the wilderness, and righteousness remain in the fruitful field. The work of righteousness will be peace, and the effect of

---

[62] *Reward*
[63] *Paradise*

righteousness, quietness and assurance forever."

8. "All the ends of the world shall remember and turn to the YAH-way."

9. "And YAH-way shall be King over all the earth. The YAH-way is one, and His name one. The kingdom is the YAH-way's, and He rules over the nations."

10. "And all the families of the Gentiles shall worship before You, for the earth will be filled with the knowledge of the glory of God, as the waters cover the sea."

11. "Hear, O earth! Blessed are the persons whom You instruct, O YAH-way, that You may give them relief from the days of adversity. For the YAH-way is good; His mercy is everlasting, and His truth[64] endures to all generations."

12. "But for every one who lives many years, and rejoices in them all, yet the days of darkness will be many. All that is coming is absurdity."

+13. "Rejoice in your youth, O young ones, and let your heart cheer you while you are young. Walk in the impulses of your heart and the pleasures of your eyes. But for all of these, remember that God will affix a price upon each of your mistakes."

14. "Remember now your Creator in the days of your youth, before the difficult days come, and the years draw near when you say, 'I have no pleasure in them.' Remove sorrow from your heart and put away evil from your flesh, for childhood and youth are nonsense."

15. "Do you not know this of old, ever since man was placed on the earth, that the triumphing of the wicked is short, and the joy of the hypocrite is but

---

[64] *Eden*

16. "But You, our God, are kind and true and patient. You rule the[65] universe with mercy. Knowing You is perfect righteousness. Recognizing Your power is where immortality begins."

17. "His blessings overflow like the Nile, enriching the world in a fertile flood."

18. "Why then are My people bent on backsliding from Me? Though they call to the Most High, none at all exalt the YAH-way."

19. "You have planted evil. You have reaped iniquity. You have eaten the fruit of lies, because you trusted in your own way."

20. "You love evil more than good, and lying rather than honest speech."

21. "When you saw a thief, you consented with him, and have been a partaker with adulterers. You give your mouth to evil. You sit and speak against your brother. You slander your own mother's son."

22. They sharpen their tongues like swords, and aim cruel words like arrows.[66]

+23. They rise early in the day and are eager to make all their deeds corrupted.

+24. "In all your behavior your sins are apparent. Your iniquities will be remembered even if you want to forget them."

25. "Repent now everyone of his evil way and his evil doings!"

---

[65] *Mistakes*
[66] *Backsliding*

26. "Be silent, all flesh, before YAH-way, for He is aroused from His holy habitation."

27. "Break up your fallow ground, and do not sow among thorns. Circumcise yourselves to the YAH-way, and take away the foreskins of your hearts."

+28. "Sow for yourselves righteousness; reap in mercy. For it is time to seek the YAH-way, till He pours His righteous teachings into you."

29. "If you will return, O Israel, return to Me. And you shall swear, 'The YAH-way lives!' in justice, and in uprightness."[67]

30. "Break off your sins and show the reality of your repentance by being truthful, and liberate yourself from your iniquities by showing mercy and loving-kindness to the poor and oppressed."

31. "Repent, and turn from all your transgressions, so that iniquity will not be your ruin."

32. "Cast away from you all the crimes you have committed, and grow a new heart and a new spirit."

33. "In their affliction they will diligently seek Me."

34. "Surely this calamity is from YAH-way. Why should I wait for the YAH-way any longer?"

35. "Does it seem good to You that You should oppress?"

36. "O you afflicted one, tossed with tempest, and not comforted, He has not despised nor abhorred the affliction of the afflicted."[68]

---

[67] *Teachings*
[68] *Liberate*

37. "If He should gather to Himself His Spirit and His breath, all flesh would perish together, and mankind would return to the dust."

38. "Who can say to Him, 'What are You doing?'"

39. "All nations before Him are as nothing, and they are counted by Him less than nothing and worthless."

40. "Woe to him who strives with his Maker! Shall the clay say to him who forms it, 'What are you making?' Or shall your handiwork say, 'She has no hands.'"

41. "Woe to those who seek deep to hide their counsel far from the YAH-way, and their works are in the dark. They say, 'Who sees us?' and, 'Who knows us?' Surely you have things turned around! Shall the potter be esteemed as the clay? For shall the thing made say of him who made it, 'He did not make me'? Or shall the thing formed say of him who formed it, 'He has no understanding'?"

42. "Can anyone tell YAH-way what to do? Who can advise the Spirit of[69] the Lord or be His teacher or give Him counsel? Whom did He consult for His enlightenment, and who taught Him the path of justice, and taught Him knowledge, and showed Him the way of understanding?"

43. "You, O son of dust, say to the children of your people: The righteousness of the righteous man shall not deliver him in the day of his transgression; as for the wickedness of the wicked, he shall not fall because of it in the day that he turns from his wickedness; nor shall the righteous be able to live because of his righteousness in the day that he sins."

+44. "When I say to the righteous that he shall surely live, but

---

[69]*Doing*

	he trusts in his own righteousness and commits iniquity, none of his righteous works shall be remembered. But because of the iniquity that he has committed, he shall be severed from Me."
+45.	"Again, when I say to the wicked, 'The peace and pleasure of your soul shall be lost,' if he turns from his sin and does what is lawful and straight, if he gives back the borrower's pledge and returns what he has stolen and walks along the paths of right, he shall surely be renewed."[70]
46.	"None of his sins that he has committed will be remembered against him. He has practiced justice and righteousness; he will be filled with life."
47.	"Yet the children of your people say, 'The way of the YAH-way is not fair.' But it is their way which is not fair!"
+48.	"When the righteous turns from his righteousness and commits iniquity, his relationship with Me shall die because of it. But when the wicked turns from his wickedness and does what is lawful and right, he shall live because of it."
+49.	"Yet you say, 'YAH-way's way is not equitable.' O house of Israel, I will judge every one of you by your individual behaviors."
50.	"Hear now, O Israel, is it not My way which is fair, and your ways which are not fair?"
+51.	"If a man begets a son who sees all the sins which his father has done, and considers but does not do likewise, he shall not be punished by Me[71] for the iniquity of his father."
+52.	"The soul who sins shall die. The child shall not bear

---

[70] *Enlightenment*
[71] *Fair*

the guilt of the parent, nor the parent bear the guilt of the child. The righteousness of the righteous shall be upon himself, and the wickedness of the wicked shall be upon himself."

+53. "Behold, all souls are Mine; the soul of the father as well as the soul of the son is Mine. The soul who sins shall be a dead soul."

+54. "But if someone is truly righteous and honest, does not approach a woman during her monthly impurity, does not seduce another man's wife, doesn't cheat or rob anyone, gives food and clothing to people who are begging, has removed himself from sinful situations and executed true justice in all his personal and business relations, this person is a just person. He shall be lonely where prevarication and pretense is approved and rewarded, but his soul shall remain alive."[72]

Nine

1. Thus saith God the YAH-way, "I will seek what was lost and bring back what was driven away, bind up the broken and strengthen what was sick; but I will destroy the fat and the strong."

2. "He will bring justice to the poor of the people. He will save the children of the needy, and will crush the oppressor."

3. "Come, and let us return to the YAH-way. For He has torn, but He will heal us; He has injured us, but He will bandage our wounds. After two days He will revive us. On the third day He will raise us up,

---

[72]*Prevarication*

that we may live in His presence."

4. "For behold, YAH-way is coming out of His place. He will come down and tread on the high places of the earth."

5. "The people have sown wheat but reaped thorns. They have put themselves to pain but do not profit. For they would not walk in His ways, nor were they obedient to His law. Was it not the YAH-way, He against whom we have sinned?"[73]

6. "You have forgotten Me and trusted in falsehood."

+7. "Salem's rulers shamefully love to say, 'Give! Give!' Why do you kick at My offering which I have commanded in My house, and honor your sons and daughters more than Me, and make yourselves fat by taking the best of the sacrifices for yourselves?"

8. "Who is blind but My servant, or deaf as My messenger whom I send? Who is blind as he who is perfect, and blind as the YAH-way's servant? Seeing many things, but you do not observe; opening the ears, but he does not hear."

---

[73]*Torn*

9. "He who kills a bull is as if he slays a man. He who sacrifices a lamb, as if he breaks a dog's neck. He who offers a grain offering, as if he offers swine's blood. He who burns incense, as if he blesses an idol."

10. "The worship of idols, whose names should never be spoken, is the beginning and the end, the cause and the result of every evil. People who worship them lose control of themselves in ecstasy, or pass off lies as prophecies, or live wickedly, or break their word without hesitation.[74] They tell lies under oath and expect no punishment, because the idols they put their trust in are lifeless."

11. Thus says the Lord GOD: "Indeed I Myself will search for My sheep and seek them out."

12. "Lo, I am sending My messenger to prepare the way before Me. And suddenly there will come to the temple the YAH-way whom you seek, and the messenger of the covenant whom you desire. Yes, he is coming."

13. But will God indeed dwell with men on the earth?

14. "Rip your heart, and not your clothes. Turn your life back to the YAH-way, your God. For He is gracious and compassionate, slow to anger and rich in kindness, and relents from doing harm."

+15. "If you return to Me, and keep My commandments and do them, and shall make My footsteps your pathway, then each judgment of yours shall be based on righteousness, and all the upright in heart will follow it."[75]

+16. "Hate insincerity and profitless pain. Love a truthful man. Be agreed and at peace in all your affairs."

17. "Rise up, you women who are at ease. Hear My voice,

---

[74]*Hesitation*
[75]*Rip*

you complacent daughters. Tremble, be troubled, strip yourselves, make yourselves bare, and gird sackcloth on your waists."

18. "Pour out your heart before God. Let tears run down like a river day and night. Pour out your heart like water before the face of the Lord."

+19. "He does not retain His anger forever, because He delights in mercylovingkindness. When we come to ourselves and repent, bring back to Him our hearts, and keep His commandments, He will again have compassion on us, and will subdue our iniquities. He will cast all our sins into the depths of the sea."

20. "For a mere moment I have forsaken you, but with great mercies I will gather you. With a little wrath I hid My face from you for a moment, but with everlasting kindness I will have mercy on you."[76]

+21. "As I have sworn that the flood before the time of Noah would never again cover the earth, so have I sworn that I would not be angry with you, nor rebuke you. For the mountains shall depart and the hills be removed, but My kindness shall not depart from you, nor shall My covenant of peace be altered."

22. "Seek the YAH-way while He may be found; call upon Him while He is near. Let the wicked leave their way of life and change their way of thinking. Let them return to YAH-way, and He will have compassion upon them. For our God is generous in forgiving."

23. "Remember your Creator before the silver cord is loosed, or the golden bowl is broken, or the pitcher shattered at the fountain, or the wheel broken at the well. Then the dust will return to the earth as it was, and the spirit will return to God who gave it."

---

[76]*Complacent*

24. "He will feed His flock like a shepherd. He will gather the lambs with His arm, and carries them close to His heart, and will gently lead those who are with young."[77]

25. "If My people who are called by My name will humble themselves, and pray and seek My face, and turn from their crooked ways, then I will hear from heaven and heal their land."

26. "Yes, let every one turn from his evil way and from the violence that is in his hands."

27. "O earth, earth, earth, hear the word of YAH-way!"

28. "The land shall not be sold permanently, because the land is Mine, and you are but strangers and sojourners with Me."

29. "I am the God who holds your hand."

30. "These are the things you shall do: Speak the truth to one another. Let there be peace and honesty in all your judgments."

+31. "You should not gloat at the adversities of another, nor speak proudly in the day of their distress."[78]

32. "Remove violence and plundering."

33. "Always be fair and honest."

34. "Stop dispossessing each other."

35. "Cast your bread upon the waters, for after many days you will find it again."

36. "Be intent to keep away from wrong, but sinners must not deny their sins. Those who say that they have not

---
[77] Bowl
[78] Gloat

	sinned against God and his majesty are only bringing fiery shame upon themselves."
37.	"Keep your tongue from speaking evil and guile."
38.	"Pursue peace. Seek it and crave it."
+39.	"Learn to do good, and be a conductor of good."
+40.	"Quit hurting other people. Make justice your aim."[79]
41.	"Encourage the oppressed and correct the oppressors."
42.	"Give help to widows and orphans."
43.	"And now, O priests, this command is for you."
44.	"Speak tenderly. Do not fear or be discouraged. Let the assembly of His faithful people praise with dancing, drums and harps."
+45.	"And the people who walk in darkness will see a great light. Upon those who have lived in the land of the shadow of death, a warm light will shine."
46.	"By the living God, who made our very souls, the YAH-way has given a commandment concerning all of us."
+47.	"Do not be wise in your own eyes. But obey the YAH-way and depart from evildoing."
48.	"Cursed is he who does the work of YAH-way deceitfully."[80]
49.	"Blessed is that man who makes the YAH-way his trust, and does not respect the proud or join along with those who easily lapse into falsehood."

---

[79] *Crave*
[80] *Tenderly*

50. "Have we not all one Father? Has not one God created us? Why do we deal treacherously with one another?"

51. "Come near, you nations, to hear; and heed, you people! Let the earth hear, and all that is in it, the world and all things that come forth from it. For the indignation of the YAH-way is against all nations, and His fury is against all their armies."

52. "For thus was the commandment of the YAH-way by his prophets in the days of old."

Ten....

1. "Sing to YAH-way, all the earth."[81]

2. "For the YAH-way is our Judge; the YAH-way is our Lawgiver; the YAH-way is our King."

3. "Come, you children, listen to me. I will teach you. Which of you desires many days of life, that he may see good yet come to him in the land of the living?"

4. "Do not envy the oppressor, and choose none of his ways. For the perverse person is an abomination to YAH-way, but His secret counsel is with the upright. He blesses the dwelling place of the just. Surely He scorns the scornful, but gives grace to the humble."

+5. "Very secret things belong to YAH-way, but those things which are revealed belong to us and to our children forever, that we may incorporate all the words of God's law into our lives."

---

[81] *Sing*

6. "The law of Your mouth is more valuable to me than thousands of shekels of silver and gold."

7. "It is better to lose your money by helping a brother or a friend than to[82] lose it by letting it rust away under a rock somewhere. Use your wealth as the Most High has commanded. This will do you more good than keeping your money for yourself."

+8. "Blessed is the one who considers the poor. The YAH-way will keep this one alive, and he or she will be blessed on the earth."

9. "But who am I, and who are my people, that we should be able to offer so willingly as this? For all things come from You, and we only give back to You what we have received. We are sojourners and transients before You."

10. "Serve the YAH-way with fear, and rejoice with trembling. Kiss His heart with your heart, lest He be angry, and you perish in the way."

+11. "Hear this, you who swallow up the needy, and make the poor of the land fail: My soul is exceedingly filled with scorn toward those who are at ease, for you have stripped the naked of their clothing, you have not given the weary water to drink, and you have withheld bread from the hungry."[83]

12. "Is it not for you to know justice?--you who hate good and love evil, who strip the skin from My people, and the flesh from their bones, who also eat the flesh of My people, flay their skin from them, break their bones, and chop them in pieces like meat for the kettle, like flesh in the caldron."

13. "I will be a swift witness against those who practice

---
[82] *Envy*
[83] *Willingly*

magic, and liars, and those who exploit widows and orphans, against those who commit adultery, and oppress the wage earner in his wages, and deprive foreigners of justice. My name is blasphemed continually every day because they do not fear Me."

14. "Hear, O you mountains, for the YAH-way has a complaint against His people."

15. "Turn, turn from your evil ways!"

16. "Behold, the whirlwind of YAH-way goes forth with fury, a sweeping whirlwind. It will fall violently on the head of the wicked."[84]

17. "It is because you have left the source of Wisdom! If you had walked in God's ways, you would have lived in peace forever."

+18. For the YAH-way can still the tumult of His people, and He can bless them with His never-ending peace.

19. "Behold, the eyes of the Lord GOD are on the sinful kingdom."

+20. "Thus you say, every one to his neighbor, 'What answer did the YAH-way give?' or, 'What did the YAH-way say?' For every one's own word has become the oracle of our God, but you make the people trust in a lie. Therefore, you shall mention no more the oracle of YAH-way, for you have perverted the words of the living God."

+21. "Thus you shall say to the prophet, 'What has YAH-way answered you?' and, 'What has YAH-way spoken?' But since she or he says, 'The prophecy of the YAH-way!' I will reply: Because you say 'The prophecy of the YAH-way!' when I have told you not to say 'The prophecy of the YAH-way!' therefore behold, I, even I, will utterly forget you and forsake you and will cast you

---

[84] *Violently*

out of My presence."[85]

22. "And I will bring an everlasting reproach upon you, and a perpetual shame, and I will destroy you from the face of the earth."

23. "I was disgusted with that generation, and said, 'It is a people who go astray in their hearts, and they do not know My ways.'"

24. "Though they say, 'As the YAH-way lives,' surely they swear falsely."

25. "O YAH-way, are not Your eyes on the truth? You have stricken them, but they have not grieved. You have consumed them, but they have refused to receive correction. They have made their faces harder than rock. You have tried to get them to be honest, but they won't change. Surely they are poor and ignorant, for they do not know the way of the YAH-way."

26. They were a stubborn and rebellious generation that did not prepare its heart aright, and whose spirit was not faithful to God.[86]

Eleven

+1. "You have daughters who hide their whoring, and your brides commit adultery. But how can I only punish them, when it is you men who meet them alone and encourage them to prostitute themselves?"

2. "Be on your guard!"

---

[85] *Tumult*
[86] *Poor*

+3.	"Whoever commits adultery lacks understanding, for both souls will begin a journey to hell."
4.	"The lips of a strange woman drip honey, and her mouth is smoother than oil, but afterwards she leaves you with nothing but bitterness and pain."
5.	"Remove thy way far from her."
6.	"Drink water from your own cistern, and rejoice with the wife of your youth. As a loving deer and a graceful doe, let her tender breasts satisfy you at all times, and always be exhilarated with her love."[87]
7.	"Why do you transgress the commandments of YAH-way, so that you cannot prosper? Because you have forsaken the YAH-way, He also has forsaken you."
8.	"This is the way of an adulterous woman: she eats and wipes her mouth, and says, 'I have done no wickedness.'"
+9.	"Because the daughters of Zion are snobs, and walk with head held high, with seductive eyes that rove among the crowds to catch the glances of men, skipping as they go, making a jingling with their feet, therefore the Lord will strike the daughters of Zion, and the YAH-way will uncover their secret body parts."
10.	"The Lord will take away the finery: the jingling anklets, the scarves, and the crescents; the pendants, the bracelets, and the veils; the headdresses, the leg ornaments, and the headbands; the perfume boxes, the charms, and the rings; the nose jewels, the outer garments, the purses and the mirrors; the fine linen and the robes. And so it shall be: instead of a sweet smell there will be a stench; instead of a sash, a rope; instead of well-set hair, baldness; instead of a rich

---

[87] *Whoring*

robe, a sackcloth skirt;[88] and a burning scar instead of beauty."

11. "The Lord **GOD** of hosts called for weeping and for mourning, but instead there is joy and gladness, slaying oxen and killing sheep, eating meat and drinking wine: 'Let us eat and drink, for tomorrow we die!'"

12. Then it was revealed in my hearing by the YAH-way, "Surely for this iniquity there will be no atonement."

13. "I will set My eyes on them for harm and not for good."

14. "Those who have hurt others with their injustice, I will punish severely."

15. "Do you think you are innocent? Have you forgotten the wickedness of your fathers, the wickedness of their wives, your own wickedness, and the wickedness of your wives, which has been committed in the land of Judah and in the streets of Jerusalem?"

+16. "Has anyone said to God, 'I have been chastened, and I will reverse my[89] offensive behavior. Teach me what I do not see. If I have done iniquity, I will do it no more'?"

17. "But no; you have dismissed the God of your salvation, and have not been mindful of the Rock of your refuge."

18. "You have cast Me off, and therefore I also have left you."

19. "What injustice have your fathers found in Me, that they have gone far from Me, have followed futilities, and have become idolaters?"

---

[88] *Snobs*
[89] *Chastened*

20. "Are you determined to walk in the paths that evil men have always followed?"

21. "O My people, what have I done to you? And how have I wearied you? Testify against Me."

+22. "But My people stand silent. Therefore, I will bring distress on them, so that they shall walk like the blind. The wisdom of their wise men shall perish, and the discernment of those who are prudent shall be hidden."[90]

23. "For the iniquity of his covetousness I was angry and struck him, because he did not remember to show mercy, but persecuted the poor and needy man, that he might even slay the broken in heart."

+24. Fearing total destruction, I said, "In the prime of my life I shall go to the gates of Sheol; I am deprived of the remainder of my years. I shall not see YAH YAH, the LORD in the land of the living; I shall observe man no more among the inhabitants of the world."

25. But then God relented.

26. "Nevertheless if you warn the wicked to turn from his way, and he does not turn from his way, he shall die in his iniquity, but you have saved your life."

27. "And now for a little while grace has been shown from the YAH-way, so that our God may enlighten our eyes and give us a measure of revival."[91]

---

[90] *Discernment*
[91] *Persecuted*

Philosophy (Ph)

One

1. "With the merciful You will show Yourself merciful; toward the loving and loyal You will show Yourself loving and loyal; toward the faithful You are faithful; toward the wholehearted You are wholehearted; toward the sincere You are sincere."

+2. "With the upright and blameless You will show Yourself upright and blameless; to the kind You are kind; to those having integrity You show Yourself having integrity; but toward the crooked and froward and devious You will be twisted and perverted and shrewd."

3. The people said, "What shall we do?"

+4. "Do not be malefactors, but seek good, so that you may live."

5. "Be strong and of good courage; do not fear nor be dismayed."

6. "The hand of our God is upon all those for good who seek Him."

+7. A man stepped forward out of the crowd, and I asked him, "Why is your[1] face sad? Are you sick? Or do you have sorrow in your heart?"

8. "Why should my face not be sad?"

9. "What is man? Of what use is he? The good that he does--the evil that he does--what does it all mean? If a person

---
[1] *Wholehearted*

lives a hundred years, he has lived an unusually long time, but compared with all eternity, those years are like a drop of water in the ocean, like a single grain of sand."

10. "You have asked a hard thing."

11. "Cast your burden on YAH-way, and He shall sustain you."

12. "Surely any human existence is vapor, a breath that passes away and does not come again."

13. "Thus my heart was grieved, and I was vexed in my mind."

+14. "I poured out my complaint before Him, and declared to Him my trouble, because my spirit was overwhelmed within me."[2]

+15. "Don't be overly concerned about the needs of your life, or what pleasures the future holds for you. Neither should you ever think that you are independent and say, 'What harm can befall me?'"

16. "When things are going well, people don't think about hard times. And when things are going badly, they forget about prosperity."

17. "Before you start criticizing, get your facts straight and think it through."

18. "Why are you cast down, O my soul? And why are you disquieted within me?"

+19. "Remember how short my time is. O God, for what futility have You created all the children of men? Who can live and not die? Who can be saved from the grave?"

---

[2]*Existence*

20. "A ship sails across the waves of the ocean, but when it is gone, it leaves no trace. A bird flies through the air, but leaves no sign that it has been there. It speeds along, riding through the thin air by the force[3] of its wings, leaving behind no trace of its passing. An arrow splits the air when it is shot at a target, but at once the air closes up behind it, and no one can tell where it passed. It is the same with us--we were born, and then we ceased to be."

21. "We finish our years like a sigh. The days of our lives are seventy years, and if by reason of strength they are eighty years, yet their boast is only labor and sorrow. For it is soon cut off, and we fly away."

22. "As for man, his days are like grass; as a flower of the field, so he flourishes. For the wind passes over it, and it is gone, and its place remembers it no more."

23. "My days are like a shadow that lengthens, and I wither away like grass."

24. "Why is light given to him who is in misery, and life to the bitter of soul, who long for death, but it does not come, and search for it more than hidden treasures, who rejoice exceedingly, and are glad when they can find the grave?"[4]

25. "Why is a man allowed to be born whom God has hedged in, and if God is only going to give him a hopeless life of uselessness and frustration?"

---

[3] *Force*
[4] *Flourishes*

26. "My sighing comes before I eat, and my groanings pour out like water. The thing I greatly feared has happened to me."

27. "If only I had died at birth, then I would have lain still and been quiet. I would have been asleep. I would have been at rest."

28. "As a father pities his children, so the YAH-way pities those who fear Him. For He understands our constitution; He remembers that we are dust."

29. "So then, don't think of anyone's life as happy until it is over, because all the evidence is not in until the person is dead."

30. "While you still live, never abandon an old friend. You will never find a new one who can take his place. When things are going well, it is hard to tell who your real friends are."

31. "Avoid idle talk, and you will avoid a lot of trouble."[5]

32. "Don't get involved in too many things. If you try to do too much, you will suffer for it. You won't be able to finish your work, and you won't be able to get away from it either. For instance, here is a man who never stops working like a slave, but gets further behind all the time. On the other hand, another man may be very poor and not up to his task. He may be slow, and he may need help, but the YAH-way is pleased with him and pulls him out of his bad situation. When he is back on his feet again, everyone is astounded."

+33. "Righteous people are nothing but a nuisance. They boast of God as their Father, and believe that only the destiny of the just will be blessed. For according to

---

[5]*Real*

	their own words, they say that God will take care of them and deliver them from the hands of their foes. But is it true? And will they still be calm and reasonable when it's time for them to die?"
+34.	"They perish forever, with no one regarding. Does not their own excellence and wisdom also die and go away?"[6]

Two

1.	"If I venture to converse with you, will you be annoyed?"
2.	"Can a mortal be more righteous than God? Can a man be more pure than his Maker?"
3.	"Choose for yourself."
4.	"Where is your life going? Can you see the path in front of you?"
5.	"Do not all go to one place, the place of the dead?"
+6.	"No one knows exactly what is to be. But I have seen the God-given task with which the children of the earth are to be occupied. I know that there is nothing better for them than to rejoice, and to do good with the years of their living."
7.	"God has made everything beautiful in its time. Also He has put eternity into man's mind, yet so that man cannot see the whole scope of God's work from

---

[6]*Destiny*

	beginning to end."[7]
+8.	"He should not dwell unduly on the short, futile days of his life, for God will keep him busy with the joy of his heart."
9.	"Let all the earth keep silence before the Merciful One."
10.	"Do you see a man hasty in his words? It is a fool who vents all his feelings, but a wise man holds them back."
11.	"He who is a patient man is better than a warrior, and he who rules his spirit is better than he who captures a city."
+12.	"If you guard your mouth and guard your tongue, you will keep your soul from troubles."
13.	"He who has knowledge spares his words, and a man of understanding is of a calm spirit."
14.	"Even a fool is thought to be wise when he is silent; when he shuts his lips, he is considered perceptive."[8]
15.	"If you are wise, you are wise for yourself, and if you scoff, you alone will bear it."
16.	"The rich man's wealth is his strong city, but wise people store up knowledge."
17.	"If the clouds are full of rain, they empty themselves upon the earth. And if a tree falls to the south or the north, in the place where the tree falls, there it shall lie. He who observes the wind will not sow, and he who regards the clouds will not reap."
18.	"The fear of the YAH-way leads to life. He who has

---

[7] *Annoyed*
[8] *Perceptive*

	it will abide in satisfaction, and will not be visited with evil."
19.	"Like a bird that wanders from its nest is a man who wanders from his place."
20.	"A man's pride causes his downfall, but a humble spirit shall obtain honor."[9]
21.	"How forceful are right words! But what does your arguing prove?"
22.	"My days are spent without hope. Remember, my life is but a breath. Our days on earth are as a shadow."
23.	"Therefore I will not restrain my mouth; I will speak in the anguish of my spirit; I will complain in the bitterness of my soul."
24.	"I would choose strangling and death rather than my body. I loathe my life. It makes no sense. I am tired of living."

---

[9] *Empty*

25.	"Should I say, 'I will forget my complaint; I will put off my sad face and wear a smile'?"
+26.	"If I am condemned to the dust, why then do I keep laboring in vain?"
27.	"For God is not a man, as I am, that I may answer Him, or go to court against Him."
28.	"If He were, then we could discuss it fairly, but there is no umpire[10] between us, no mediator to bring us together."
29.	"Your hands have made me and fashioned me, an intricate unity; yet You would destroy me!"
+30.	"My soul hates my life. I will give free course to the expression of my perturbations."
31.	Then I said to the earth, "Look at what you

---

[10]*Tired*

	have done! When you gave birth to the rest of creation, you gave birth to reason."
32.	"What good is it for any of us to have life in the present age, when it is full of misery, and when all we can look forward to after death is worms and punishment for our sins?"
33.	I said to myself: "I must search for wisdom and try to understand. I was brought into this world without my consent, and I will leave it against my will. God has given me only a few short years as my span of life."[11]
+34.	"We raise our daughters and sons by teaching them the righteousness of God's laws, and we discipline them."
+35.	"You are the Creator and, as You wish, You can take away a life or allow us to live."
36.	"But if You are so ready to destroy a person that was so carefully created, WHY WAS HE CREATED IN THE FIRST PLACE?"
+37.	"Judge me, O God, according to the integrity of my inward parts, and according to the straightness of my life."
38.	"How long shall I take counsel in my soul, having sorrow in my heart daily?"
39.	"Bring my soul out of prison. Consider and hear me. Enlighten my eyes."[12]

---

[11] *Mediator*
[12] *Straightness*

Three

1. "Shall a multitude of words go unanswered? And should a man full of talk be vindicated? When you mock, should no one rebuke you?"

+2. "You claim you are pure in the sight of God, and that your unhappiness is unjustified."

3. "But are you not also guilty before YAH-way, your God?"

4. "Oh, that God would speak; that He would show you His secrets and double your prudence. Know for a certainty that God exacts from you less than your iniquity deserves."

5. "He does not punish us according to our sins, nor requite us for all of our many hurtful doings."

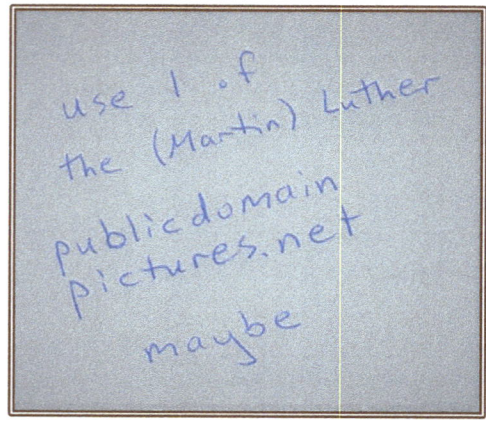

+6. "If You, YAH, should mark our iniquities, O Lord, who could stand?"

7. "Wisdom is the principal thing. Therefore, get wisdom, and in all your getting, get understanding. Exalt her, and she will promote you. She[13] will bring

---
[13] *Vindicated*

	you honor when you embrace her. She will place on your head an ornament of grace."
8.	"You would also lie down, and none would disturb you. Yes, many would court your favor. For good understanding gains favor."
9.	"If you search for good you will find favor, but trouble will come to him who seeks evil."
10.	"He who disdains instruction despises his own soul."
11.	"Whoever hides hatred has lying lips, and whoever spreads accusations is a wild beast."
12.	"There is one who scatters, yet increases more. And there is one who withholds more than is right, but it leads to poverty."
13.	"Whoever loves wisdom makes his father glad, but he who associates with prostitutes wastes his wealth."[14]
14.	"An empty-headed man will be wise when a wild donkey's colt is born a man."
15.	"Evil people are trapped in their own sins, while honest people are happy and free."
+16.	"Treasures of wickedness profit nothing, but an honest heart will do two things: it will save you from having a dead heart, and it will deliver you from the fear of bodily death."
17.	"When there is strife, and a contention arises, remember that the beginning of strife is like releasing water. Therefore, stop contention before a quarrel starts."

---

[14] *Ornament*

18.	"Even if you have a violent argument with a friend, and speak sharply, all is not lost. You can still be reconciled. But any friend will leave you if you insult him, if you are arrogant, if you reveal his secrets, or if you turn on him unexpectedly."
19.	"He who forgives a transgression promotes trust, but whoever repeats a[15] matter separates the best of friends."
+20.	"Folly is joy to him who is destitute of discernment, but a man of understanding walks sublimely."
21.	"By long forbearance a ruler is persuaded, and a gentle tongue breaks a bone."
+22.	"Do not exalt yourself in the presence of the king, and do not stand in the place of great men. For it is better that he says to you, 'Come up here,' than to be put lower while other men are watching."
23.	"Consider what you should do."
24.	"And in all that I have said to you, be circumspect."[16]

Four--Darius

1.	"No doubt you are the man, and wisdom will die with you! But I have understanding as well as you. I am not inferior. Indeed, who does not know such things as these?"
2.	"Now hear my reasoning, and heed the pleadings of my lips."

---

[15] *Empty-headed*
[16] *Watching*

3. "Does not the ear test words? As the tongue can distinguish the flavors of different kinds of meat, so a sharp mind can detect insincere words."

4. "Will you speak wickedly for God, and talk deceitfully for Him? Will you contend for God? Will it be well when He examines you? Do you think you can fool God the way you fool men?"

5. "Man that is born of a woman is of few days and full of turmoil. He comes forth like a flower and fades away. He flees like a shadow, and continues not."

+6. "How nice it would be if I were hidden in the grave at this moment."[17]

7. "If a man dies, shall he live again? All the days of my hard service I will wait, till my change comes."

8. "As water wears away stones, and as torrents wash away the soil of the earth, so You, O Lord GOD, destroy the hope of man. You prevail forever against him, and he passes on; You change his countenance and send him away."

9. "Absurdity of absurdities! All is nonsense. What profit has a man from all his labor in which he toils under the sun?"

10. "One generation passes away, and another generation comes. The sun also rises, and the sun goes down, and hastens to the place where it arose."

---

[17]*Turmoil*

11.	"The wind goes toward the south, and turns around to the north. The wind whirls about continually, and on its circular courses the wind returns. All the rivers run into the sea, yet the sea is not full. To the place from which the rivers come, there they go again."[18]
+12.	"Everything is a mundane and wearisome rigmarole."
+13.	"But people prefer to pretend it is not true."
14.	"The eye is not satisfied with seeing, nor the ear filled with hearing."
15.	"That which has been is what will be. That which is done is what will be done. And there is nothing new under the sun."
16.	"Is there anything of which it may be said, 'See, this is new'? No, it has all happened before in the ages that preceded us."
17.	"There is no remembrance of former things, nor will there be any remembrance of things that are to come by those who will come after."
18.	"Many years ago, I, Darius, set my heart to seek and search out by wisdom all the things that are done in this world. I have seen all the works that are done under the sun; and indeed, it is all a futile effort, like chasing the wind."[19]
19.	"What is crooked cannot be made straight, and what is lacking cannot be counted."

---

[18] *Circular*
[19] *Rigmarole*

20.	"And I set my heart to know wisdom and to know madness and folly. I perceived that this also is grasping for the wind. Because in much wisdom there is much grief, and he who increases knowledge increases sorrow."
+21.	"I communed with my heart, saying, 'Come now, I will make a test of pleasure; enjoy yourself.' But behold, this also was frustrating. I said of laughter, 'It is madness'; and of mirth, 'What does it accomplish?'"
22.	"I searched in my heart how to gratify my flesh, while guiding my heart with wisdom, till I might see what was good for the sons of men to do under heaven all the days of their lives."
23.	"I undertook great projects. I built myself houses. I made myself gardens and orchards, and I planted all kinds of fruit trees in them. I acquired male and female servants, and had servants born in my house."[20]
24.	"I also gathered for myself silver and gold and the special treasures of kings and of the provinces. I acquired male and female singers, the delights of the sons of men, and musical instruments of all kinds. So I became great and excelled more than all who were before me in Jerusalem. Also my wisdom remained with me."
25.	"Whatever my eyes desired I did not keep from them. I did not withhold my heart from any pleasure. For my heart rejoiced in

---

[20] *Frustrating*

	all my labor, and this was my reward. Then I looked on all the works that my hands had done and on the labor in which I had toiled, and behold, all was vanity and worthless and of no value."
+26.	"So I turned again to consider what is wise and what is insane and what is utterly ridiculous."
27.	"Then I saw that wisdom excels folly as light excels darkness. The wise man's eyes are in his head, but the fool walks in darkness. Yet I myself perceived that the same event happens to them all."
+28.	"So I said in my heart, 'As it happens to one who runs blindly, it also[21] happens to me. Why then do I consider myself wiser?' Then I said in my heart, 'This is absurd as well.'"
29.	"For there is no more remembrance of the wise than of the fool forever, since all that now is will be forgotten in the days to come. And how does a wise man die? As the fool! Therefore, I hated life."
30.	"Moreover I saw: in the place of justice, wickedness was there; and in the place of righteousness, iniquity was there. I also thought, 'As for men, God tests them so that they may see that they are like the animals. All go to one place. All are from the dust, and all return to dust.'"
+31.	"Who can tell whether our spirits go elsewhere than where the animals go?"
32.	"So I perceived that there is nothing better

---

[21] *Insane*

than that a man should rejoice in his own works, for that is his best portion. For who can bring him to see what will happen after him?"[22]

33. "There is a nonsense which occurs on earth: there are just men treated as though they had done evil and wicked men treated as though they had done justly. I said that this also is vanity. So I commended enjoyment, because a man has nothing better under the sun than to eat, drink, and be merry."

34. "I have been young, and now am old, yet I have not seen the righteous forsaken, nor his descendants begging bread; but you will not believe it even if I tell you."

35. "Man is like a breath. His days are like a passing shadow."

36. "Then I returned and considered all the oppression that is done under the sun. And look! The tears of the oppressed, but they have no comforter. And on the side of their oppressors was power, but they too had no comforter."

37. "Therefore I praised the dead who were already dead, more than the living who are still alive. Yet, better than both is he who has never existed."[23]

38. "Again, I saw that for all toil and every skillful work a man is envied by his neighbor. This also is nonsense."

39. "There is an evil which I have seen under the sun, and it is common among men. If a

---
[22] *Absurd*
[23] *Bread*

	man begets a hundred children and lives many years, but his soul is not satisfied with goodness, or indeed he has no burial, I say that a stillborn child is better than he. For it comes in vain, and goes into obscurity, and its name is covered with darkness. Though it has not seen the sun or known anything, this has more rest than an old man, even if he lives a thousand years twice over, but has not seen goodness in his life."
+40.	"When I applied my heart to know wisdom and to see the business that is done on earth, I spent an eon of effort; all to no avail."
41.	"For though a man labors to discover it, yet he will not find it. Moreover, though a wise man attempts to know it, he will not be able."[24]

Five

1.	"Should a wise man answer with empty knowledge, and fill himself with the east wind? Should he reason with unprofitable talk, or by speeches with which he can do no good?"
2.	"Are the consolations of God too small for you, and the word gently spoken? Why does your heart carry you away, and what do your eyes wink at, that you turn your spirit against God, and let such words go out of your mouth?"
3.	"The wisdom of the prudent will consider the consequences of what they say. Fools say whatever

---
[24]*Toil*

	comes to mind. Wise people think before they speak."
4.	"Learn where understanding, strength, and insight are to be found. Then you will know where to find a long and full life, light to guide you, and peace."
+5.	"Fearing the YAH-way is the first step toward loving Him, and faith is the first step toward being loyal to Him."[25]
+6.	"If you see the government oppressing the poor, and the violent perversion of justice and truth in a province, do not marvel at this, for anxiety in the heart causes depression, but a good word makes it glad."
7.	"A merry heart does good, like medicine, but a broken spirit dries the bones."
+8.	"Do not be overly honest and good, nor be overly intelligent: why should you destroy yourself? Nor be overly wicked or mindless: why should you die before your time? It will be helpful if you can grasp this."
9.	"Human beings are like leaves on a spreading tree. New growth takes the place of the fallen leaves; while some of us die, others are being born. Everything made by human hands will decay and perish, along with the person who made it."
10.	"A wooden beam can be put into a building so firmly that an earthquake cannot shake it loose. A person can be trained to use reason and good sense so well that he keeps his head when a crisis comes."[26]
11.	"Be careful when somebody offers you

---

[25] *Consequences*
[26] *Medicine*

	advice. Find out first what his interest in the matter is, because you can be sure that he is thinking primarily of himself."
12.	"There is no cure for the troubles that arrogant people have; wickedness has taken deep root in them. Intelligent people will learn from proverbs and parables. They listen well because they want to learn."
13.	"Wisdom is the book of God's commandments. Turn to Wisdom, and take hold of her. Make your way toward the splendor of her light."
+14.	"No one has seen God. No one can describe Him. No one can praise Him properly. We know only a fraction of His works. The Lord made the universe and then gave wisdom to devout men."
15.	"Obey Him."
16.	"Do justice and righteousness."
+17.	"YAH-way hates all forms of evil, and those who take the YAH-way[27] seriously are not attracted to evil. When He created human beings, He left them free to do as they wished. If you want to, you can keep the Lord's commands. You can decide whether you will be loyal to Him or not."
18.	"Go in peace."
19.	"How long till you put an end to words? Gain understanding, and afterward we will speak."
20.	"Like one who takes away a garment in cold weather is one who sings songs to a heavy heart."

---

[27] *Thinking*

21. "If I say to corruption, 'You are my father,' and to the worm, 'You are my mother and my sister,' where then is my hope?"

22. "Though I speak, my grief is not relieved; and if I remain silent, how am I eased?"

23. "Oh, that one might plead for a man with God, as a man pleads for his[28] friend!"

24. "Is my complaint against man?"

25. "Why do the wicked live and become old, yes, become mighty in power? Their descendants are established with them in their sight, and their offspring before their eyes."

26. "Their houses are safe from fear, neither is the rod of God upon them. Their bull breeds without failure; their cow calves without miscarriage. They send forth their little ones like a flock, and their children dance."

27. "They sing to the tambourine and harp, and rejoice to the sound of the flute. They spend their days in wealth, and without lingering go down to the grave."

28. "Yet they say to God, 'Depart from us, for we do not desire the knowledge of Your ways. Who is the Almighty, that we should serve Him? And what profit do we have if we pray?'"[29]

29. "So I was perplexed when I saw how You tolerate sinners and do not punish them, how You protect Your enemies and yet

---

[28] Eased
[29] Breeds

	destroy Your own people."
30.	"No other nation, except Israel, has ever known You or accepted Your covenants. But Israel was never rewarded, and never profited from its labor. I have traveled widely in the other nations, and I have seen how prosperous they are, although they don't keep Your commands."
31.	"Now then, Lord, if You would just weigh our sins on the scales against those of the rest of the world, it would be perfectly clear that their sins are heavier. There has never been a time when the people of the world did not sin against You, but has any other nation kept Your commands as well as Israel has? You may find individuals who have, but You won't find a nation that has done so."
32.	"It would have been better if we had never been born than to have to live in a world of sin and suffering without understanding why things happen as they do."[30]

Six....

1.	"Just as trees have their place on land, and waves have their place in the sea, so the people of this world can understand only what goes on in this world, and only heavenly beings can understand what goes on in heaven."

---
[30] *Perplexed*

2.   "Why then was I given the ability to understand anything? I am always troubled whenever I try to think about the ways of God Most High or to understand even a small part of what He does."

3.   "You cannot understand!"

4.   "Why not, sir? In that case, why was I born? Why didn't I die before I was born?"

5.   "If you live long enough, you will be surprised at what you will see."

6.   He continued, "Picture in your mind a broad, immense sea spreading over a vast area, but with an entrance no wider than a river. No one who wishes to enter that sea, whether to visit it or control it, can reach[31] its broad expanse of water without passing through the narrow entrance."

7.   "Or take another example: picture a city built on a plain. The city is full of all kinds of good things, but the entrance to it is narrow and steep, with fire on one side and deep water on the other. The one path between the fire and the water is so narrow that only one person at a time may walk on it. If anyone inherits this city, he cannot take possession of his inheritance without passing through this dangerous entrance."

8.   "Only a few people are righteous, and there are large numbers of wicked people. But listen: if you had only a few precious stones, would you add lumps of lead and clay to them in order to have more?"

9.   "And I will put My Spirit within you, and you will come to life."

---

[31] *Heavenly*

10.		"The YAH-way tests the righteous."
+11.		"But the wicked and the ones who love violence His soul hates, for they[32] do not speak peace, but they devise methods of deceit against those who are quiet in the land."
12.		"His merciful kindness is great toward us, and the truth of YAH-way endures forever, even like the faithful witness in the sky."
+13.		"God declares to man His thoughts in our thoughts."
14.		"O man greatly beloved, fear not! Peace be to you; be strong, yes, be strong!"
15.		"One dies in his full strength, being wholly at ease and secure. His pails are full of milk, and the marrow of his bones is moist. Another man dies in the bitterness of his soul, never having eaten with pleasure. They lie down alike in the dust, and worms cover them."
16.		"How then can you comfort me with empty words, since falsehood remains in your answers?"
+17.		"While I was still young, I began to seek the God of David and our[33] ancestors. And God gave me good deliberation skills and the ability to judge equitably, and largeness of heart like the sand on the seashore. My wise-mindedness excelled that of all the men of the East and all the wisdom of Egypt. For I was wiser than all men--than Ethan the Ezrahite, and Heman, Chalcol, and Darda, the sons of Mahol; and my fame

---

[32] *Narrow*
[33] *Marrow*

was in all the surrounding nations."

+18. "I spoke three thousand proverbs, and have written one thousand and five songs. Wisdom was my teacher. She taught me about the nature of living creatures, the behavior of wild animals, the force of the winds, the reasoning powers of human beings, the different kinds of plants, and the use of their roots as medicine. I learned things that were well known, and things that had never been known before."

+19. "By Her power and under Her authority, I learned true knowledge of the forces of nature: what the world is made of, how the elements behave, how the calendar is determined by the movements of the sun, the changing seasons, the constellations, and the cycles of years."

+20. "I learned of trees, from the cedar tree of Lebanon even to the hyssop[34] that springs out of the wall. I learned also of animals, of birds, of creeping things, and of fish. And men of all nations, from all the kings of the earth, came to hear my words."

21. "I thought to myself: Because of Her I will be honored wherever people come together. The old men will respect me, even though I am young. They will find that my opinions show deep insight, and those in power will admire me. When I am silent, they will wait for me to speak, and when I speak, they will pay attention. Even when I speak at length, they will listen with concentration."

+22. "Even if a man is perfect, he will be thought of as nothing without the Wisdom that

---

[34] *Constellations*

	comes from You. You chose me over everyone else to be the leader of Your own people, to judge Your sons and daughters. You told me to build a temple, an altar in Jerusalem. It is an earthly copy of Your heavenly temple."
23.	"Like the moon, I am full--full of more ideas to be discussed."
+24.	"I examined the wisdom of all the ancient writers. I memorized the[35] sayings of famous men. I studied the hidden meaning of proverbs and was able to discuss the obscure points of parables. I traveled to foreign lands in my effort to learn about human good and evil. I had knowledge to share and good advice to give, as well as insight into the Lord's secrets. I used to think I would die a famous man, and if I died before I had become famous, I would still be pleased and content."
+25.	"Yes, that's what I used to think."

Seven--Zerubbabel

+1.	"One time I gave a great banquet. I invited all the members of my family and staff. I also invited three young men who I knew to be knowledgeable and skilled in all literature and wisdom. In matters of intelligence I knew them to be ten times better than all the magicians and astrologers in our land."

---

[35]*Concentration*

+2. "When everyone had had enough to eat and drink, we moved to the[36] sitting room."

3. "Then the three young men said to one another, 'Let each one of us name the one thing that he considers the strongest thing in the world.' Then each of them wrote down the best answer he could think of."

4. "The first wrote, 'There is nothing stronger than wine.' The second wrote, 'There is nothing stronger than the emperor.' And the third wrote, 'There is nothing stronger than a woman, but truth can conquer anything.'"

+5. "I had the three statements read aloud. Then I said to the three young men, 'Please explain your answers.'"

6. "The man who had written about the strength of wine spoke first: 'Wine is clearly the strongest thing in the world. It confuses the mind of everyone who drinks it. It has exactly the same effect on everyone: king or orphan, slave or free, rich or poor. It makes every thought happy and carefree, and makes one forget every sorrow and responsibility. It makes everyone feel rich, ignore the power of kings[37] and officials, and talk as if he owned the whole world. When men drink wine, they forget who their friends and neighbors are, and then they are soon drawing their swords to fight them. Then, when they sober up, they don't remember what they have done. If wine makes men act in this way, it certainly must be the strongest thing in the world.'"

---

[36] *Literature*
[37] *Explain*

7. "The man who had written about the strength of the emperor spoke next. 'Nothing in the world is stronger than men, since they rule over land and sea and, in fact, over everything in the world. But the emperor is the strongest of them all; he is their lord and master, and men obey him, no matter what he commands. If he tells them to make war on one another, they do it. If he sends them out against his enemies, they go, even if they have to break down mountains, walls, or towers. They may kill or be killed, but they never disobey the emperor's orders. If they are victorious, they bring him all their loot and everything else they have taken in battle. Farmers do not go out to war, but even they bring to the emperor a part of everything that they harvest, and they pay taxes to the emperor. Although the emperor is only one man, if he orders people to kill, they kill; if he orders them to set prisoners free, they do it; if he orders them to attack, they do; if he[38] orders destruction, they destroy; if he orders them to build, they build; if he orders crops to be destroyed or fields to be planted, it is done. Everybody, soldier or civilian, obeys the emperor. And when he sits down to eat or drink and then falls asleep, his servants stand guard around him, without being able to go and take care of their own affairs. Since people obey the emperor like this, certainly nothing in the world is stronger than he is.'"

8. "The man who had written about women and the truth--his name was Zerubbabel--spoke last. 'The emperor is certainly powerful, men are numerous, and

---

[38] Farmers

wine is strong, but who rules and controls them all? It is women! Women gave birth to the emperor and all the men who rule over land and sea. Women brought them into the world. Women brought up the men who planted the vineyards from which wine comes. Women make the clothes that men wear; women bring honor to men; in fact, without women, men couldn't live. Men may accumulate silver or gold or other beautiful things, but if they see a woman with a pretty face or a good figure, they will leave it all to gape and stare, and they will desire her more than their wealth. A man will leave his own father, who brought him up, and leave his own country[39] to get married. He will forget his father, his mother, and his country to spend the rest of his life with his wife. So you must recognize that women are your masters. Don't you work and sweat and then take all that you have earned and give it to your wives? A man will take his sword and go out to attack, rob and steal, and sail the seas and rivers. He may have to face lions or travel in the dark, but when he has robbed, stolen, and plundered, he will bring the loot home to the woman he loves. A man loves his wife more than his parents. Some men are driven out of their minds on account of a woman, and others become slaves for the sake of a woman. Others have been put to death, have ruined their lives, or have committed crimes because of a woman. So now do you believe me? The emperor's power is certainly great--no nation has the courage to attack him. But once I saw him with Apame, his concubine, the daughter of the famous Bartacus. While sitting at the

---

[39] *Zerubbabel*

emperor's right, she took his crown off his head, put it on her own, and then slapped his face with her left hand. All the emperor did was look at her with his mouth open. Whenever she smiles at him, he smiles back; and when she gets angry with him, he flatters her and teases her until she is in a good mood again. If women can do all that, surely there can be nothing stronger in the world.'"[40]

+9. "At this point, all of us in the room just looked at one another."

10. "Then Zerubbabel began to speak about truth. 'Yes,' he said, 'women are very strong. But think of how big the earth is, how high the sky is; think how fast the sun moves, as it rapidly circles the whole sky in a single day. If the sun can do this, it is certainly great. But truth is greater and stronger than all of these things. Everyone on earth honors truth; heaven praises it; all creation trembles in awe before it. There is not the slightest injustice in truth. You will find injustice in wine, the emperor, women, all human beings, in all they do, and in everything else. There is no truth in them; they are unjust and they will perish. But truth endures and is always strong; it will continue to live and reign forever. Truth shows no partiality or favoritism; it does what is right, rather than what is unjust or evil. Everyone approves what truth does; its decisions are always fair. Truth is strong, royal, powerful, and majestic forever. Let all things praise the God of truth!' When Zerubbabel had finished speaking, all the people shouted, 'Truth is great--there is

---

[40] *Apame*

		nothing stronger!'"
11.		"Then the young man Zerubbabel looked up to heaven. 'Lord, all praise[41] belongs to You. You are the source of all victory and wisdom, and I thank You, O Lord of our ancestors, for giving wisdom to me, Your servant.'"
12.	Meditation.	
+13.		"Some time after this event, I sent out a letter for distribution to many places, in which was written a collection of wise saws. As I recall to my mind, here are some of the things that I included in it."
14.		"To all peoples, nations and languages that dwell in all the earth: peace be multiplied to you. Who can ever learn the will of God? Human reason is not adequate for the task, and our philosophies tend to mislead us, because our mortal bodies weigh our souls down. The body is a temporary structure made of earth, a burden to the active mind."
15.		"I realized that I would never receive Wisdom unless God gave Her to me--and knowing that only God could give Her to me was itself a sign of understanding. So I prayed, begging the Lord with all my heart: God of my ancestors, merciful Lord, by Your word You created[42] everything."
16.		"All we can do is make guesses about things on earth; we must struggle to learn about things that are close to us. Who, then, can ever hope to understand heavenly things? No one has ever learned Your will,

---

[41] *Big*
[42] *Philosophies*

	unless You first gave him Wisdom, and sent Your holy spirit down to him. In this way people on earth have been set on the right path, have learned what pleases You, and have been kept safe by Wisdom."
17.	"If you receive my words, and treasure my commands within you, and apply your heart to understanding; yes, if you cry out for discernment, and search for her as for hidden treasures, then you will understand the fear of the YAH-way. For YAH-way gives wisdom; from His mouth come knowledge and understanding. He is a shield to those who walk uprightly, and He preserves the way of His saints."[43]

Eight

1.	"You shall teach these words diligently to your children, and shall talk of them when you sit in your house, when you walk, when you lie down, and when you rise up. Bind them at your wrist as a sign and let them be as a pendant on your forehead. Write them on the doorposts of your houses and on your gates."
2.	"Bind them on your fingers. Write them on the tablet of your heart. Say to wisdom, 'You are my sister,' and call understanding your intimate friend."
3.	"Diligence is man's precious possession."

---

[43] *Heart*

4. "The heart of the wise teaches his mouth, and adds learning to his lips."

5. "Cease listening to instruction, my people, and you will stray from the words of knowledge."

6. "Do not trust in oppression, nor vainly hope in robbery. If riches increase, do not set your heart on them."[44]

7. "A good name is to be chosen rather than great riches, and loving favor rather than silver and gold."

8. "Better is a little with righteousness, than vast revenues without justice."

9. "Better is a dry morsel with quietness, than a house full of feasting with strife."

10. "Don't miss your chance to marry a wise and good woman. A gracious wife is worth more than gold."

11. "If you have a good wife, do not divorce her, but do not trust yourself to someone you don't love."

12. "Better is a dinner of vegetables where love is, than a fatted calf with hatred."

13. "It is better to be poor, but strong and healthy, than to be rich, but in poor health. The finest food means nothing if you are too sick to eat it.[45] The afflicted man looks at his food and sighs, like a castrated man hugging a girl."

---

[44] *Learning*
[45] *Loving*

+14. "Who has found the place of Wisdom? Who has entered into Her treasure house? Many who have tried have vanished: the rulers of the nations, the men who hunted wild animals and birds for sport, those who accumulated fortunes of silver and gold in which everyone trusts and will do anything to get. But these have not found where Wisdom lives."

15. "It is better to have virtue, even if it means having no children. Virtue provides an example for people to follow; when it is not there, they miss it."

16. "Do not overwork to be rich; because of your own understanding, cease! Will you set your eyes on that which is not? For riches certainly make themselves wings; they fly away like an eagle."

17. "He who hates covetousness and unjust gain shall prolong his days."[46]

18. "The wise shall inherit glory, but shame shall be the legacy of fools."

19. "He who is devoid of wisdom despises his neighbor, but a smart man will keep quiet."

20. "The rich rules over the poor, and the borrower is servant to the lender."

21. "As in water face reveals face, so a man's heart reveals the man."

+22. "Those who shame the counsel of the poor do not realize that YAH-way is his refuge. Rich men are conceited and think they are wise, but a poor person who has insight can

---

[46] Treasure

	see past the facade."
23.	"In the day of prosperity be joyful, but in the day of adversity consider: God has made them both."
+24.	"He who loves silver will not be satisfied with silver, and whoever is covetous of wealth will always think he needs more."
25.	"Wisdom is a defense as money is a defense, but the excellence of[47] knowledge is that wisdom gives life to those who have it."
26.	"Giving to the poor can make up for sin, just as water can put out a blazing fire. Anyone who responds to others with acts of kindness is thinking of the future, because he will find help if he ever falls on hard times."
27.	"Keep your self-respect, but remain modest. Value yourself at your true worth. There is no excuse for a person to run himself down. No one respects a person who has no respect for himself."
28.	"Take advantage of opportunities, but guard yourself against evil. Don't underrate yourself. Humility deserves honor and respect, but a low opinion of yourself leads to sin."
29.	"Do not let others have their way at your expense; do not bring on your own ruin by giving up your rights. Never hesitate to speak out when the occasion calls for it. Don't hide your wisdom."[48]

---

[47] *Facade*
[48] *Underrate*

Nine

1. "Many important truths have been handed down to us, and we should praise Israel for the instruction and wisdom they provide. But it is not enough that those who read them should gain understanding for themselves. Anyone who values learning should be able to help others by what he himself says and writes."

2. "If you appreciate wisdom when you hear it, you will become wise yourself, and your words will be a source of wisdom for others."

3. "Your wisdom and education can be known only by what you say. Do not, however, go against the truth, and remember that you do not know everything."

4. "Put Wisdom's chains around your feet and Her yoke around your neck. Carry Her on your shoulders and don't be resentful of Her bonds. Follow Wisdom, and keep to Her ways with all your heart."

5. "You can learn if you want to. You can be clever if you are determined to be. If you are willing to listen, you will learn and[49] become wise."

6. "Be careful in everything you do. When sin is all around you, be especially careful that you do not become guilty."

---
[49] *Education*

7. "Every creature prefers its own kind, and people are no different. Just as animals of the same species flock together, so people keep company with people like themselves."

8. "A wise person will not speak until the right moment, but a bragging fool doesn't know when that time is. No one can stand a person who talks too long and will not give others a chance to speak."

9. "Some people keep quiet because they don't have anything to say; others keep quiet because they know the right time to speak."

10. "A person can be rebuked in the wrong way; it may be wiser to keep quiet than to speak. But it is much better to rebuke the person than to keep your anger bottled up."[50]

11. "Explaining something to a fool is like explaining it to a sleepy man. When you have finished, he'll say, 'What was that again?'"

+12. "When wicked people curse their enemies they are really cursing themselves."

13. "When an educated person hears something that shows insight, it stimulates his mind and leads him on to other ideas. But when someone who is satisfied with ignorance hears it, he won't like it, and will forget it as soon as he can."

14. "Lying is an ugly blot on a person's character, but ignorant people do it all the time."

---

[50] Bragging

15.	"Foolish people are always contradicting themselves. When you find yourself with stupid people, look for some excuse to leave, but when you are with serious-minded people, stay as long as you can."
+16.	"Do not speak in the hearing of persons who are steeped in mendacity, for they will always despise the wisdom of your words."[51]
17.	"People hate a person who has nothing but scorn for others."
18.	"The schemes of folly are sin, and there is no justice when a witness is determined to hurt someone."
19.	"Do not say, 'I will do to him just as he has done to me.'"
20.	"It is better to listen to the rebuke of the wise than for a man to hear the song of fools."
21.	"Remember that death is coming for you some day, and you haven't been told when that will be. Before that day comes, be kind to your friends; be as generous as you can. Don't deny yourself a single day's happiness. If there is something you want to do and it is lawful, go ahead!"
22.	"Some day all that you have worked for will be divided up and given to others. So be generous; but also be willing to receive from others. Enjoy yourself, for you will not find

---

[51] *Ugly*

	any pleasures in the world of the dead."[52]
+23.	"I applied my heart to know, to search and seek out wisdom and the reason of things; and to convince myself that trying to achieve selfish benefits by dishonest methods is not possible."
+24.	"Here is what I have discovered, adding one thing to another to find an explanation: No woman knows how to be sincere, and only one man out of a thousand is upright in his dealings. Though my soul still seeks."
25.	"And the woman whose heart is snares and nets I find more bitter than death. Her arms are chains. He who is good before God can get away, but the sinner will be captured by her."
26.	"A man who lives for nothing but sexual enjoyment will keep on until that fire destroys him. To such a man all women are desirable, and he can never get enough as long as he lives."
+27.	"When you go out to find a desirable woman to be with, do not ask another woman for advice about her rival."[53]
28.	"A gracious wife is her husband's delight."
29.	"A loud-mouthed, talkative woman is like a trumpet sounding the signal for attack, and any man who has such a wife will spend his life at war."
30.	"No poison is deadlier than the poison of a

---

[52] *Generous*
[53] *Possible*

	snake, and no anger is deadlier than the anger of a woman. I would rather live in the same house with a lion or a dragon than with a bad wife."
31.	"When a wife is in a bad mood, her expression changes until she looks like an angry bear. Her husband has to go and eat with the neighbors, where he can't hold back his bitter sighs. Compared with the troubles caused by a woman, any other trouble looks small."
32.	"A continual dripping on a very rainy day and a contentious woman are alike."
33.	"A quiet man living with a nagging wife is like an old man climbing up a sandy hill."[54]

Ten....

1.	"Many people have sinned while looking for a profit. If you want to be rich, you have to keep blinders on your eyes."
2.	"A person who gets rich without sinfully chasing after money is fortunate. Do you know anyone like that? If so, we will congratulate him for performing a miracle that no one else has ever been able to do. If anyone has ever passed this test, he can well be proud."
3.	"Has anyone ever known that he could get away with cheating someone, and not taken advantage of it? If so, he deserves his

[54]*Talkative*

	wealth, and everyone will praise him for his generosity."
+4.	"The weapons of a rogue are evil. He devises wicked schemes to destroy the afflicted with slander, even though it is the needy one who speaks justly."
5.	"He who is noble, open-hearted and liberal devises noble things, and by noble plans he stands. An honorable person acts honestly and will be generous to others."[55]
6.	"The desire of the slothful kills him, for his hands refuse to labor. He covets greedily all day long, but the righteous gives without sparing."
7.	"It is better to work and have more than you need than to go around boasting but hungry."
8.	"Those slain by the sword are better off than those who die of hunger."
9.	"With his lips an enemy speaks sweetly, but in his heart he plots how to trap you. While you stand firm, he makes no bold move, but if you slip, you will find him waiting, ready to trip you up while he pretends to help you."
+10.	"He will nod his head, rub his hands, spread rumors about you, and show his true face. Though he acts like he can feel your pain, he will kill you if he gets a chance."
11.	"Don't live the life of a beggar; it is better to die than to beg. If you have to depend on

---

[55] *Honestly*

someone else for your food, you are not really living your own life. You pollute yourself by accepting food from another[56] person."

+12. "People who are shameless can make begging sound like fun, but something in their inward feelings burns like fire."

+13. "When the righteous become great, the people rejoice, but when a wicked man rules, the people groan. For a wicked leader is lazy and won't put his shoulders to work helping the people."

14. "A wise ruler will educate his people, and his government will be orderly. All the officials and all the citizens will be like their ruler. An uneducated king will ruin his people, but a government will grow strong if its princes have wisdom."

+15. "There are many examples of rulers who misuse their power, not only in the stories that have been handed down to us from the past, but we still hear of outrageous things happening every day. The only way to make sure that a kingdom remains untroubled and peaceful is by changing policies which encourage exploitation, and by judging fairly in each situation."[57]

16. "Ointment and perfume delight the heart, and the sweetness of a man's friend does so by earnest counsel of the soul."

17. "As iron sharpens iron, so a man sharpens the countenance of his friend by a stimulating discussion."

---

[56] *Waiting*
[57] *Outrageous*

18.	"He who rebukes a man will find more favor afterward than he who flatters with the tongue."
+19.	"Wisdom is better than weapons of war, but the folly of one sinner can upend a mountain of good."
20.	"If the ax is dull, and one does not sharpen the edge, then he must use more strength; but wisdom brings success."
21.	"When you make a vow to God, do not delay to pay it; for He has no pleasure in fools. Pay what you have vowed. It is better not to vow than to promise you will do something and then not do it."
22.	"Also do not take to heart every bitter thing people say about you, for[58] you know that you likewise have many times cursed others."
+23.	"A godly person who rejects her faith in a high-pressure situation is like a murky spring or an impure fountain."
24.	"If you are chosen to preside at a banquet, don't put on airs. Just be like everyone else. Look after the guests before you sit down. After you have performed your duties, you can sit down and enjoy yourself with the others. They will respect you for doing a good job. If you are older than most of the guests, you may talk; that is your right. But you should know what you are talking about and not interrupt the music. If entertainment is being provided, don't keep up a steady conversation; it's the wrong

---

[58] *Stimulating*

	time to show off your wit."
+25.	"Music at a banquet where wine is served is like a ruby set in gold; if the music is good and the wine is good--even better!"
26.	"Leave the party at the right time and never be the last to go. Don't linger at the door; just go straight home."[59]
27.	"On your way, if you meet anyone, do not greet him. And if anyone greets you, do not answer him."
+28.	"Heed your own heart's counsel, for what do you have that is more dependable than that? Sometimes a man's intuition can tell him more than seven watchmen on a high tower."
29.	"But don't be too sure of yourself, even when the way looks easy."
30.	"Protect your reputation; it will outlive you and last longer than a thousand treasures of gold."
31.	"Never do anything without thinking it through, and once you have done something, don't look back and wish you had done something else."
32.	"I pray to God that my thoughts may be worthy of what I have learned, and that I may speak according to His will. He is Wisdom's guide; He gives correction to those who are wise."
33.	"Do not be afraid when one becomes rich,

---

[59]*Murky*

when the glory of his house[60] is increased. For when he dies he shall carry nothing away; his glory shall not descend after him. Though while he lives he blesses himself (for men will praise you when you do well for yourself), he shall go to the generation of his fathers. They shall never see the light of life. Man who is in honor, yet does not understand, is like the beasts that perish."

Eleven

+1. "O precious YAH-way, teach us to number our days, that we may gain a heart of clear-sighted intelligence."

+2. "I urge you to read these words carefully and often, and with an open mind. Some of these thoughts have been translated from other languages and, in spite of all my diligent efforts, I may not have translated some phrases very well. That is true not only of these words, but even of the Piety stories, the Prophecy stories, and the others. The translation can differ quite a bit from the original. Always be patient[61] and listen for the deeper spirit behind the words."

+3. "Thus ended my letter. At a younger age, I was convinced that a man who did not make God his strength, but trusted in the abundance of his worldly riches, was continuously making a bad choice."

---

[60]*Dependable*
[61]*Translated*

4. "But now I see: All man's efforts are for his mouth, yet his appetite is never satisfied. What advantage has a wise man over a fool? What does a poor man gain by knowing how to conduct himself before others? Better what the eye sees than the roving of the appetite; yet both are meaningless in the end."

5. "Surely men of low degree are a vapor; men of high degree are a lie. If they are weighed in the balances, they are altogether lighter than vapor."

6. "Who is the wise man who may understand this? And who is he to whom the mouth of the YAH-way has spoken, that he may declare it?"

+7. "Your prophets have seen for you false and deceptive visions. They[62] have not uncovered your iniquity, but have envisioned for you untrue teachings and delusions."

8. "Wise men die. Likewise, the fool and the senseless person perish, and leave their wealth to others."

+9. "I have seen all things during my futile days of this silly life."

10. "Now if it is not so, who will prove me a liar, and make my speech worth nothing?"

11. "O YAH-way, what is man, that You are mindful of him?"

12. "For a thousand years in Your sight are like yesterday when it is past."

---

[62] *Appetite*

13.	"Oh, send out Your light and Your truth! Let them lead me."
14.	"Oh, that I knew where I might find Him!"
15.	"You have set your words in order before me. You have taken your[63] stand."
16.	"Let us know. Let us pursue the knowledge of the YAH-way, that we may be enlightened with the light of life."
17.	"Have I not wept for him who was in trouble? Has not my soul grieved for the poor? But when I looked for good, evil came to me."
+18.	"If I have rejoiced at the destruction of him who hated me, or hypocritically sworn an oath, saying, 'As the YAH-way lives,' O LORD, deliver my soul from my lying lips and from having a deceitful tongue."
19.	"Death and life are in the power of the tongue."
20.	"I hate and despise lying."
21.	"Deliver me from the deceitful and unjust man!"
22.	"Oh, that I had one to hear me!"[64]
23.	"Give me understanding, and I shall live."
24.	"When YAH-way spoke through His prophets, the people made fun of them and laughed."

---

[63] *Envisioned*
[64] *Life*

+25. "I have given symbols and parables through the witness of the prophets."

26. "But the great things of My law were considered a strange thing."

Twelve--The Preacher

+1. "Sir Darius, maybe your heart was proud because of your beauty, and you corrupted your wisdom for the sake of your splendor."

+2. "What did you hope to gain by despising the quiet day of small things?"

3. "The ear tests words as the palate tastes food. Let us choose justice for[65] ourselves. Let us know among ourselves what is good."

4. "Do you say, 'My righteousness is more than God's'?"

+5. "Can a vigorous man be profitable to God? Though perhaps he who is wise may be profitable to himself. Is it any pleasure to the Almighty that you are just and not deceitful? Or is it of any benefit to Him that you think your ways are blameless?"

6. "Bear with me a little."

7. "Has the rain a father? Or who has begotten the drops of dew? From whose womb comes the ice? And the frost of heaven, who gives it birth?"

8. "Who has measured the waters in the hollow of his

---
[65]*Darius*

	hand? And calculated the dust of the earth? Or weighed the mountains and the hills in a balance?"
9.	"I urge you to look at the sky and the earth. Consider everything you[66] see there, and realize that God made it all from nothing."
+10.	"Where can wisdom be found? And where is the place of understanding? Man does not know its value, nor is it to be found among women."
11.	"It cannot be purchased with gold, for the price of wisdom is above rubies."
12.	"Indeed these are the mere edges of His ways. How small a whisper we hear of Him!"
13.	"Surely I have calmed and quieted my soul, like a weaned child within me."
+14.	"In You I take refuge. When my insides are filled with anxiety, Your comforts delight my soul."
15.	"I think of You during the night, when I remember You on my bed."[67]
16.	"YAH-way knows the thoughts of all people."
17.	"Be very humble, because the decay of death awaits us all."
18.	"When a person dies, all he then possesses is worms, flies, and maggots."
19.	"We are only dust and ashes. What have we got to be proud of? Our body decays even while we are alive."
20.	"Grief lingers on after the death of a loved one, but it

---

[66] *Calculated*
[67] *Edges*

is not wise to let it lead you into poverty. Weep bitterly and passionately; observe the proper period of mourning for the person. Mourn for a whole day or maybe two, to keep people from talking, but then pull yourself together and reconcile yourself to the loss. You will die, just as he did. Today it was his turn; tomorrow it will be yours. There is no way to bring the dead person back. All your sorrow does him no good, and it hurts you. Don't forget that."

21. "Shout joyfully before the YAH-way, the King."[68]

22. "Your statutes have been my songs in the house of my pilgrimage."

23. "Your counsels of old are faithfulness and truth."

24. "You, through Your commandments, make me wiser than my enemies."

25. "Good and upright is the YAH-way; therefore, He teaches sinners in the way. The humble He guides in justice, and the humble He teaches in prudence. All the paths of the YAH-way are mercy and truth, to those who abide by His testimonies."

26. "For YAH-way loves justice, and does not abandon His saints," says the Preacher.

+27. Then Darius understood again what he had perhaps forgotten during the long years of his life.

28. "I thought about my ways, and turned my feet. I made haste, and did not delay to keep Your commandments."[69]

29. "For You are my lamp, O YAH-way. The YAH-way shall enlighten my darkness."

---

[68] *Passionately*
[69] *Pilgrimage*

30.	"Make me understand the way of Your precepts."
31.	"Make me walk in the path of Your commandments, for I delight in it."
32.	"Therefore I will look to the LORD. When I sit in darkness, YAH-way will be a light to me."
33.	"I will meditate on Your laws, and contemplate Your teachings."
34.	"I will walk with the YAH-way in the world of the living."
35.	"In Him my soul shall make its boast."
36.	"I will be his Father, and he shall be My son; and I will not take My mercy away from him."
37.	"You rescue me from violent men. Therefore, I will give thanks to You[70] among the Gentiles, and sing praises to Your name."
38.	"You have comforted me, and have spoken kindly."
+39.	"Blessed be all people of the YAH-way who do not forsake His kindness to the living and the dead!"[71]

---

[70] *Meditate*
[71] *Blessed*

Works Cited

Folly & Iniquity

accumulating	www.lulu.com/shop/mike-marty/accumulating/ebook/product-23589196.html (Retrieved 4/14/25)
arguments	www.lulu.com/shop/mike-marty/arguments/ebook/product-23589172.html (Retrieved 4/14/25)
astray	www.lulu.com/shop/mike-marty/astray/ebook/product-23589149.html (Retrieved 4/14/25)
Athaliah	www.lulu.com/shop/mike-marty/athaliah/ebook/product-23589127.html (Retrieved 4/14/25)
bronze	www.lulu.com/shop/mike-marty/bronze/ebook/product-23592385.html (Retrieved 4/14/25)
business	www.lulu.com/shop/mike-marty/business/ebook/product-23592375.html (Retrieved 4/14/25)
cartwheel	www.lulu.com/shop/mike-marty/cartwheel/ebook/product-23586502.html (Retrieved 4/14/25)
contrive	www.lulu.com/shop/mike-marty/contrive/ebook/product-23586492.html (Retrieved 4/14/25)
corrupt	www.lulu.com/shop/mike-marty/corrupt/ebook/product-23586484.html (Retrieved 4/14/25) https://youtu.be/LbOycbA7Bq8
cunning	www.lulu.com/shop/mike-marty/cunning/ebook/product-23586477.html (Retrieved 4/14/25)
demand	www.lulu.com/shop/mike-marty/demand/ebook/product-23585245.html (Retrieved 4/14/25)
desperately	www.lulu.com/shop/mike-marty/desperately/ebook/product-23585225.html (Retrieved 4/14/25)
disdained	www.lulu.com/shop/mike-marty/disdained/ebook/product-23585195.html (Retrieved 4/14/25)
disobedient	www.lulu.com/shop/mike-marty/disobedient/ebook/product-23585176.html (Retrieved 4/14/25) https://youtu.be/pJgQINmN2gs
ditch	www.lulu.com/shop/mike-marty/ditch/ebook/product-23583475.html (Retrieved 4/14/25)
evil	www.lulu.com/shop/mike-marty/evil/ebook/product-23583451.html (Retrieved 4/14/25)
exorbitant	www.lulu.com/shop/mike-marty/exorbitant/ebook/product-23583443.html (Retrieved 4/14/25)
fascinated	www.lulu.com/shop/mike-marty/fascinated/ebook/product-23583432.html (Retrieved 4/14/25)
forgers	www.lulu.com/shop/mike-marty/forgers/ebook/product-23580728.html (Retrieved 4/14/25)
fortunetellers	www.lulu.com/shop/mike-marty/fortunetellers/ebook/product-23580716.html (Retrieved 4/14/25)
gentleman	www.lulu.com/shop/mike-marty/gentleman/ebook/product-23573213.html (Retrieved 4/14/25) https://youtu.be/IUITkEP9QpY
haters	www.lulu.com/shop/mike-marty/haters/ebook/product-23567212.html (Retrieved 4/14/25)
hoarded	www.lulu.com/shop/mike-marty/hoarded/ebook/product-23563867.html (Retrieved 4/14/25)
illusions	www.lulu.com/shop/mike-marty/illusions/ebook/product-23559764.html (Retrieved 4/14/25)
imagination	www.lulu.com/shop/mike-marty/imagination/ebook/product-23555244.html (Retrieved 4/14/25)
lasciviously	www.lulu.com/shop/mike-marty/lasciviously/ebook/product-23551045.html (Retrieved 4/14/25)
lattice	www.lulu.com/shop/mike-marty/lattice/ebook/product-23547485.html (Retrieved 4/14/25)
linger	www.lulu.com/shop/mike-marty/linger/ebook/product-23542043.html (Retrieved 4/14/25)
lurking	www.lulu.com/shop/mike-marty/lurking/ebook/product-23538213.html (Retrieved 4/14/25)
monster	www.lulu.com/shop/mike-marty/monster/ebook/product-23534904.html (Retrieved 4/14/25)
nonsense	www.lulu.com/shop/mike-marty/nonsense/ebook/product-23530217.html (Retrieved 4/14/25)
oblivion	www.lulu.com/shop/mike-marty/oblivion/ebook/product-23526085.html (Retrieved 4/14/25)
oppose	www.lulu.com/shop/mike-marty/oppose/ebook/product-23523590.html (Retrieved 4/14/25)
perpetually	https://www.kobo.com/us/en/ebook/perpetually (Retrieved 4/14/25)
platitudes	www.lulu.com/shop/mike-marty/platitudes/ebook/product-23516051.html (Retrieved 4/14/25)
plaything	www.lulu.com/shop/mike-marty/plaything/ebook/product-23511330.html (Retrieved 4/14/25)
pounce	www.lulu.com/shop/mike-marty/pounce/ebook/product-23507505.html (Retrieved 4/14/25)
prickly	www.lulu.com/shop/mike-marty/prickly/ebook/product-23504934.html (Retrieved 4/14/25)
prowl	www.lulu.com/shop/mike-marty/prowl/ebook/product-23499462.html (Retrieved 4/14/25)
reconsider	www.lulu.com/shop/mike-marty/reconsider/ebook/product-23495932.html (Retrieved 4/14/25)
religious	www.lulu.com/shop/mike-marty/religious/ebook/product-23491965.html (Retrieved 4/14/25)
renounce	www.lulu.com/shop/mike-marty/renounce/ebook/product-23487581.html (Retrieved 4/14/25)
revolt	www.lulu.com/shop/mike-marty/revolt/ebook/product-23483641.html (Retrieved 4/14/25)

sarcastic	www.lulu.com/shop/mike-marty/sarcastic/ebook/product-23479090.html (Retrieved 4/14/25)
Sheol	www.lulu.com/shop/mike-marty/sheol/ebook/product-23474688.html (Retrieved 4/14/25)
springtime	www.lulu.com/shop/mike-marty/springtime/ebook/product-23456560.html (Retrieved 4/14/25)
stricken	www.lulu.com/shop/mike-marty/stricken/ebook/product-23453405.html (Retrieved 4/14/25)
superficially	www.lulu.com/shop/superficially/ebook/product-23410706.html (Retrieved 4/14/25)
sympathy	www.lulu.com/shop/mike-marty/sympathy/ebook/product-23448778.html (Retrieved 4/14/25)
timid	www.lulu.com/shop/mike-marty/timid/ebook/product-23443421.html (Retrieved 4/14/25)
unrighteousness	www.lulu.com/shop/mike-marty/unrighteousness/ebook/product-23438729.html (Retrieved 4/20/25)
uproar	www.lulu.com/shop/mike-marty/uproar/ebook/product-23435288.html (Retrieved 4/20/25)
venom	www.lulu.com/shop/mike-marty/venom/ebook/product-23428336.html (Retrieved 4/20/25)
wave	www.lulu.com/shop/mike-marty/wave/ebook/product-23423849.html (Retrieved 4/20/25)
whirlwind	www.lulu.com/shop/mike-marty/whirlwind/ebook/product-23419564.html (Retrieved 4/20/25)
Zodiac	www.lulu.com/shop/mike-marty/zodiac/ebook/product-23414707.html (Retrieved 4/20/25)

Prophecy

abolished	www.lulu.com/shop/mike-marty/abolished/ebook/product-23767012.html (Retrieved 4/20/25)
acknowledges	www.lulu.com/shop/mike-marty/acknowledges/ebook/product-23768491.html (Retrieved 4/20/25)
advantage	www.lulu.com/shop/mike-marty/advantage/ebook/product-23771171.html (Retrieved 4/20/25)
alarmed	www.lulu.com/shop/mike-marty/alarmed/ebook/product-23771163.html (Retrieved 4/20/25)
ashamed	www.lulu.com/shop/mike-marty/ashamed/ebook/product-23777605.html (Retrieved 4/20/25)
avenge	www.lulu.com/shop/mike-marty/avenge/ebook/product-23764630.html (Retrieved 4/20/25)
babblers	www.lulu.com/shop/mike-marty/babblers/ebook/product-23762076.html (Retrieved 4/20/25)
backbite	www.lulu.com/shop/mike-marty/backbite/ebook/product-23762067.html (Retrieved 4/20/25)
backsliding	www.lulu.com/shop/mike-marty/backsliding/ebook/product-23762040.html (Retrieved 4/20/25)
bloodshed	www.lulu.com/shop/mike-marty/bloodshed/ebook/product-23758443.html (Retrieved 4/20/25)
bowl	www.lulu.com/shop/mike-marty/bowl/ebook/product-23756805.html (Retrieved 4/20/25)
boys	www.lulu.com/shop/mike-marty/boys/ebook/product-23756798.html (Retrieved 4/20/25)
chastened	www.lulu.com/shop/mike-marty/chastened/ebook/product-23750059.html (Retrieved 4/20/25)
coastlands	www.lulu.com/shop/mike-marty/coastlands/ebook/product-23749158.html (Retrieved 4/20/25)
complacent	www.lulu.com/shop/mike-marty/complacent/ebook/product-23746032.html (Retrieved 4/20/25)
crave	www.lulu.com/shop/mike-marty/crave/ebook/product-23741568.html (Retrieved 4/20/25)
dastard	www.lulu.com/shop/mike-marty/dastard/ebook/product-23739632.html (Retrieved 4/20/25)
degenerate	www.lulu.com/shop/mike-marty/degenerate/ebook/product-23739567.html (Retrieved 4/20/25)
discernment	www.lulu.com/shop/mike-marty/discernment/ebook/product-23735180.html (Retrieved 4/20/25)
dismissed	www.lulu.com/shop/mike-marty/dismissed/ebook/product-23735189.html (Retrieved 4/20/25)
doing	www.lulu.com/shop/mike-marty/doing/ebook/product-23732777.html (Retrieved 4/20/25)
Eden	www.lulu.com/shop/mike-marty/eden/ebook/product-23728495.html (Retrieved 4/20/25)
enlightenment	www.lulu.com/shop/mike-marty/enlightenment/ebook/product-23723216.html (Retrieved 4/20/25)
entertainer	www.lulu.com/shop/mike-marty/entertainer/ebook/product-23723209.html (Retrieved 4/20/25)
envy	www.lulu.com/shop/mike-marty/envy/ebook/product-23723183.html (Retrieved 4/20/25)
fair	www.lulu.com/shop/mike-marty/fair/ebook/product-23720307.html (Retrieved 4/20/25)
fig	www.lulu.com/shop/mike-marty/fig/ebook/product-23717572.html (Retrieved 4/20/25)
flint	www.lulu.com/shop/mike-marty/flint/ebook/product-23715861.html (Retrieved 4/20/25)
gloat	www.lulu.com/shop/mike-marty/gloat/ebook/product-23710158.html (Retrieved 4/20/25)
grasshoppers	www.lulu.com/shop/mike-marty/grasshoppers/ebook/product-23707533.html (Retrieved 4/20/25)
Haggai	www.lulu.com/shop/mike-marty/haggai/ebook/product-23705321.html (Retrieved 4/20/25)
handiwork	www.lulu.com/shop/mike-marty/handiwork/ebook/product-23705312.html (Retrieved 4/20/25)
hardships	www.lulu.com/shop/mike-marty/hardships/ebook/product-23704406.html (Retrieved 4/20/25)
harmful	www.lulu.com/shop/mike-marty/harmful/ebook/product-23704387.html (Retrieved 4/20/25)
haughtiness	www.lulu.com/shop/mike-marty/haughtiness/ebook/product-23704379.html (Retrieved 4/20/25)
hesitation	www.lulu.com/shop/mike-marty/hesitation/ebook/product-23701488.html (Retrieved 4/20/25)
holes	www.lulu.com/shop/mike-marty/holes/ebook/product-23699082.html (Retrieved 4/20/25)
hook	www.lulu.com/shop/mike-marty/hook/ebook/product-23804874.html (Retrieved 4/20/25)
hopeless	www.lulu.com/shop/mike-marty/hopeless/ebook/product-23699024.html (Retrieved 4/20/25)
housetop	www.lulu.com/shop/mike-marty/housetop/ebook/product-23697425.html (Retrieved 4/20/25)
hungry	www.lulu.com/shop/mike-marty/hungry/ebook/product-23695596.html (Retrieved 4/20/25)
hurl	www.lulu.com/shop/mike-marty/hurl/ebook/product-23695583.html (Retrieved 4/20/25)
inexhaustible	www.lulu.com/shop/mike-marty/inexhaustible/ebook/product-23692886.html (Retrieved 4/20/25)
inherited	www.lulu.com/shop/mike-marty/inherited/ebook/product-23691545.html (Retrieved 4/20/25)
interceded	www.lulu.com/shop/mike-marty/interceded/ebook/product-23688883.html (Retrieved 4/20/25)
Israel	www.lulu.com/shop/mike-marty/israel/ebook/product-23686967.html (Retrieved 4/20/25)
land	https://www.amazon.com/dp/B0757ZPRQT (Retrieved 4/20/25)
liberate	www.lulu.com/shop/mike-marty/liberate/ebook/product-23683289.html (Retrieved 4/20/25)

loosen	www.lulu.com/shop/mike-marty/loosen/ebook/product-23679992.html (Retrieved 4/20/25)
mistakes	www.lulu.com/shop/mike-marty/mistakes/ebook/product-23672730.html (Retrieved 4/20/25)
mysterious	www.lulu.com/shop/mike-marty/mysterious/ebook/product-23672686.html (Retrieved 4/20/25)
nourish	www.lulu.com/shop/mike-marty/nourish/ebook/product-23668015.html (Retrieved 4/20/25)
overflowing	www.lulu.com/shop/mike-marty/overflowing/ebook/product-23664560.html (Retrieved 4/20/25)
parables	www.lulu.com/shop/mike-marty/parables/ebook/product-23664535.html (Retrieved 4/20/25)
Paradise	www.lulu.com/shop/mike-marty/paradise/ebook/product-23664498.html (Retrieved 4/20/25)
patient	www.lulu.com/shop/mike-marty/patient/ebook/product-23661915.html (Retrieved 4/20/25)
persecuted	www.lulu.com/shop/mike-marty/persecuted/ebook/product-23658803.html (Retrieved 4/20/25)
perversity	www.lulu.com/shop/mike-marty/perversity/ebook/product-23658790.html (Retrieved 4/20/25)
poor	https://www.amazon.com/dp/B0774S4SWV (Retrieved 4/20/25)
presumptuous	www.lulu.com/shop/mike-marty/presumptuous/ebook/product-23654031.html (Retrieved 4/20/25)
prevarication	www.lulu.com/shop/mike-marty/prevarication/ebook/product-23652383.html (Retrieved 4/20/25)
reckoned	www.lulu.com/shop/mike-marty/reckoned/ebook/product-23649790.html (Retrieved 4/20/25)
repentant	www.lulu.com/shop/mike-marty/repentant/ebook/product-23648206.html (Retrieved 4/20/25)
reprove	www.lulu.com/shop/mike-marty/reprove/ebook/product-23645202.html (Retrieved 4/20/25)
reward	www.lulu.com/shop/mike-marty/reward/ebook/product-23642805.html (Retrieved 4/20/25)
rip	https://www.lulu.com/shop/mike-marty/rip/ebook/product-23641285.html (Retrieved 4/20/25)
secrets	www.lulu.com/shop/mike-marty/secrets/ebook/product-23635468.html (Retrieved 4/20/25)
serpent	www.lulu.com/shop/mike-marty/serpent/ebook/product-23633398.html (Retrieved 4/20/25)
shouting	https://www.amazon.com/dp/B0776R422D (Retrieved 4/20/25)
shrub	www.lulu.com/shop/mike-marty/shrub/ebook/product-23630941.html (Retrieved 4/20/25)
sing	www.lulu.com/shop/mike-marty/sing/ebook/product-23628065.html (Retrieved 4/20/25)
slaughter	www.lulu.com/shop/mike-marty/slaughter/ebook/product-23628027.html (Retrieved 4/20/25)
snobs	www.lulu.com/shop/mike-marty/snobs/ebook/product-23628000.html (Retrieved 4/20/25)
startle	www.lulu.com/shop/mike-marty/startle/ebook/product-23623658.html (Retrieved 4/20/25)
straight	www.lulu.com/shop/mike-marty/straight/ebook/product-23623677.html (Retrieved 4/20/25)
stray	www.lulu.com/shop/mike-marty/stray/ebook/product-23622724.html (Retrieved 4/20/25)
stripped	www.lulu.com/shop/mike-marty/stripped/ebook/product-23622709.html (Retrieved 4/20/25)
teachings	www.lulu.com/shop/mike-marty/teachings/ebook/product-23617270.html (Retrieved 4/20/25)
tenderly	www.lulu.com/shop/mike-marty/tenderly/ebook/product-23617259.html (Retrieved 4/20/25)
torn	https://www.lulu.com/shop/mike-marty/torn/ebook/product-23613374.html (Retrieved 4/20/25)
travailed	www.lulu.com/shop/mike-marty/travailed/ebook/product-23610481.html (Retrieved 4/20/25)
treacherously	www.lulu.com/shop/mike-marty/treacherously/ebook/product-23610444.html (Retrieved 4/20/25)
tumult	www.lulu.com/shop/mike-marty/tumult/ebook/product-23606948.html (Retrieved 4/20/25)
turn	https://www.lulu.com/shop/mike-marty/turn/ebook/product-23606935.html (Retrieved 4/20/25)
uncircumcised	www.lulu.com/shop/mike-marty/uncircumcised/ebook/product-23605842.html (Retrieved 4/20/25)
violently	www.lulu.com/shop/mike-marty/violently/ebook/product-23600332.html (Retrieved 4/20/25)
wailed	www.lulu.com/shop/mike-marty/wailed/ebook/product-23600293.html (Retrieved 4/20/25)
weaned	www.lulu.com/shop/mike-marty/weaned/ebook/product-23598902.html (Retrieved 4/20/25)
whoring	www.lulu.com/shop/mike-marty/whoring/ebook/product-23595726.html (Retrieved 4/20/25)
why	https://www.lulu.com/shop/mike-marty/why/ebook/product-23592784.html (Retrieved 4/20/25)
willingly	www.lulu.com/shop/mike-marty/willingly/ebook/product-23592781.html (Retrieved 4/20/25)

Philosophy

absurd	www.lulu.com/shop/mike-marty/absurd/ebook/product-23767034.html (Retrieved 4/21/25)
annoyed	www.lulu.com/shop/mike-marty/annoyed/ebook/product-23773927.html (Retrieved 4/21/25)
Apame	www.lulu.com/shop/mike-marty/apame/ebook/product-23775000.html (Retrieved 4/21/25)
appetite	www.lulu.com/shop/mike-marty/appetite/ebook/product-23775007.html (Retrieved 4/21/25)
big	https://www.lulu.com/shop/mike-marty/big/ebook/product-23760923.html (Retrieved 4/21/25)
blessed	www.lulu.com/shop/mike-marty/blessed/ebook/product-23758456.html (Retrieved 4/21/25)
bragging	www.lulu.com/shop/mike-marty/bragging/ebook/product-23755159.html (Retrieved 4/21/25)
bread	www.lulu.com/shop/mike-marty/bread/ebook/product-23755119.html (Retrieved 4/21/25)
breeds	https://www.amazon.com/dp/B0777PMMJN (Retrieved 4/21/25)
calculated	www.lulu.com/shop/mike-marty/calculated/ebook/product-23752640.html (Retrieved 4/21/25)
circular	https://www.amazon.com/dp/B07572H7VJ (Retrieved 4/21/25)
concentration	www.lulu.com/shop/mike-marty/concentration/ebook/product-23746008.html (Retrieved 4/21/25)
consequences	www.lulu.com/shop/mike-marty/consequences/ebook/product-23743510.html (Retrieved 4/21/25)
constellations	www.lulu.com/shop/mike-marty/constellations/ebook/product-23743495.html (Retrieved 4/21/25)
Darius	www.lulu.com/shop/mike-marty/darius/ebook/product-23741556.html (Retrieved 4/21/25)
dependable	www.lulu.com/shop/mike-marty/dependable/ebook/product-23737075.html (Retrieved 4/21/25)
destiny	www.lulu.com/shop/mike-marty/destiny/ebook/product-23737042.html (Retrieved 4/21/25)
eased	www.lulu.com/shop/mike-marty/eased/ebook/product-23730202.html (Retrieved 4/21/25)
edges	www.lulu.com/shop/mike-marty/edges/ebook/product-23792850.html (Retrieved 4/21/25)
education	www.lulu.com/shop/mike-marty/education/ebook/product-23728477.html (Retrieved 4/21/25)
empty	www.lulu.com/shop/mike-marty/empty/ebook/product-23726308.html (Retrieved 4/21/25)
empty-headed	www.lulu.com/shop/mike-marty/empty-headed/ebook/product-23726234.html (Retrieved 4/21/25)
envisioned	www.lulu.com/shop/mike-marty/envisioned/ebook/product-23723196.html (Retrieved 4/21/25)
existence	www.lulu.com/shop/mike-marty/existence/ebook/product-23721959.html (Retrieved 4/21/25)
explain	www.lulu.com/shop/mike-marty/explain/ebook/product-23721950.html (Retrieved 4/21/25)
facade	www.lulu.com/shop/mike-marty/facade/ebook/product-23720302.html (Retrieved 4/21/25)
farmers	www.lulu.com/shop/mike-marty/farmers/ebook/product-23717610.html (Retrieved 4/21/25)
flourishes	www.lulu.com/shop/mike-marty/flourishes/ebook/product-23715850.html (Retrieved 4/21/25)
force	www.lulu.com/shop/mike-marty/force/ebook/product-23715835.html (Retrieved 4/21/25)
frustrating	www.lulu.com/shop/mike-marty/frustrating/ebook/product-23711362.html (Retrieved 4/21/25)
generous	www.lulu.com/shop/mike-marty/generous/ebook/product-23711353.html (Retrieved 4/21/25)
heart	www.lulu.com/shop/mike-marty/heart/ebook/product-23704397.html (Retrieved 4/21/25)
heavenly	www.lulu.com/shop/mike-marty/heavenly/ebook/product-23701528.html (Retrieved 4/21/25)
honestly	www.lulu.com/shop/mike-marty/honestly/ebook/product-23699067.html (Retrieved 4/21/25)
insane	www.lulu.com/shop/mike-marty/insane/ebook/product-23691507.html (Retrieved 4/21/25)
learning	www.lulu.com/shop/mike-marty/learning/ebook/product-23683315.html (Retrieved 4/21/25)
life	https://www.lulu.com/shop/mike-marty/life/ebook/product-23683263.html (Retrieved 4/21/25)
literature	www.lulu.com/shop/mike-marty/literature/ebook/product-23680016.html (Retrieved 4/21/25)
loving	www.lulu.com/shop/mike-marty/loving/ebook/product-23678742.html (Retrieved 4/21/25)
marrow	www.lulu.com/shop/mike-marty/marrow/ebook/product-23676704.html (Retrieved 4/21/25)
mediator	www.lulu.com/shop/mike-marty/mediator/ebook/product-23676680.html (Retrieved 4/21/25)
medicine	www.lulu.com/shop/mike-marty/medicine/ebook/product-23674118.html (Retrieved 4/21/25)
meditate	www.lulu.com/shop/mike-marty/meditate/ebook/product-23674082.html (Retrieved 4/21/25)
murky	www.lulu.com/shop/mike-marty/murky/ebook/product-23672709.html (Retrieved 4/21/25)
narrow	www.lulu.com/shop/mike-marty/narrow/ebook/product-23672669.html (Retrieved 4/21/25)
ornament	www.lulu.com/shop/mike-marty/ornament/ebook/product-23666979.html (Retrieved 4/21/25)
outrageous	www.lulu.com/shop/mike-marty/outrageous/ebook/product-23666926.html (Retrieved 4/21/25)
passionately	www.lulu.com/shop/mike-marty/passionately/ebook/product-23661957.html (Retrieved 4/21/25)

perceptive	www.lulu.com/shop/mike-marty/perceptive/ebook/product-23661122.html (Retrieved 4/21/25)
perplexed	www.lulu.com/shop/mike-marty/perplexed/ebook/product-23661103.html (Retrieved 4/21/25)
philosophies	www.lulu.com/shop/mike-marty/philosophies/ebook/product-23658749.html (Retrieved 4/21/25)
pilgrimage	www.lulu.com/shop/mike-marty/pilgrimage/ebook/product-23655836.html (Retrieved 4/21/25)
possible	www.lulu.com/shop/mike-marty/possible/ebook/product-23654048.html (Retrieved 4/21/25)
real	https://www.lulu.com/shop/mike-marty/real/ebook/product-23649837.html (Retrieved 4/21/25)
rigmarole	www.lulu.com/shop/mike-marty/rigmarole/ebook/product-23642812.html (Retrieved 4/21/25)
stimulating	www.lulu.com/shop/mike-marty/stimulating/ebook/product-23623688.html (Retrieved 4/21/25)
straightness	www.lulu.com/shop/mike-marty/straightness/ebook/product-23622735.html (Retrieved 4/21/25)
talkative	www.lulu.com/shop/mike-marty/talkative/ebook/product-23619927.html (Retrieved 4/21/25)
thinking	www.lulu.com/shop/mike-marty/thinking/ebook/product-23617239.html (Retrieved 4/21/25)
tired	https://www.lulu.com/shop/mike-marty/tired/ebook/product-23614169.html (Retrieved 4/21/25)
toil	https://www.lulu.com/shop/mike-marty/toil/ebook/product-23614187.html (Retrieved 4/21/25)
translated	www.lulu.com/shop/mike-marty/translated/ebook/product-23610403.html (Retrieved 4/21/25)
treasure	www.lulu.com/shop/mike-marty/treasure/ebook/product-23610426.html (Retrieved 4/21/25)
turmoil	www.lulu.com/shop/mike-marty/turmoil/ebook/product-23606924.html (Retrieved 4/21/25)
ugly	https://www.lulu.com/shop/mike-marty/ugly/ebook/product-23605807.html (Retrieved 4/21/25)
underrate	www.lulu.com/shop/mike-marty/underrate/ebook/product-23605778.html (Retrieved 4/21/25)
vindicated	www.lulu.com/shop/mike-marty/vindicated/ebook/product-23600355.html (Retrieved 4/21/25)
waiting	www.lulu.com/shop/mike-marty/waiting/ebook/product-23598968.html (Retrieved 4/21/25)
watching	www.lulu.com/shop/mike-marty/watching/ebook/product-23598917.html (Retrieved 4/21/25)
wholehearted	www.lulu.com/shop/mike-marty/wholehearted/ebook/product-23595762.html (Retrieved 4/21/25)
Zerubbabel	www.lulu.com/shop/mike-marty/zerubbabel/ebook/product-23592392.html (Retrieved 4/21/25)

www.ingramcontent.com/pod-product-compliance
Lightning Source LLC
Chambersburg PA
CBHW052031030426
42337CB00027B/4951